ACHIEVING
EYPS

Applied Social Science for Early Years

ACHIEVING
EYPS

Applied Social Science for Early Years

Ewan Ingleby
and
Geraldine Oliver

Series editors: Lyn Trodd and Gill Goodliff

LearningMatters

First published in 2008 by Learning Matters Ltd

British Library Cataloguing in Publication Data
A CIP record for this book is available from the British Library

ISBN 978 1 84445 172 2

Cover design by Phil Barker
Text design by Code 5 Design Associates Ltd
Project Management by Swales & Willis Ltd
Typeset by Kelly Gray
Printed and bound by TJ International Ltd, Padstow, Cornwall

Learning Matters
33 Southernhay East
Exeter EX1 1NX
Tel: 01392 215560
info@learningmatters.co.uk
www.learningmatters.co.uk

FSC
Mixed Sources
Product group from well-managed forests and other controlled sources
Cert no. SGS-COC-2482
www.fsc.org
© 1996 Forest Stewardship Council

Contents

About the authors and series editors

Ewan Ingleby

Ewan Ingleby is a Senior Lecturer in Education/Early Years at the University of Teesside. Alongside contributing to the University of Teesside's education programmes, Ewan has been involved with teacher training at Sunderland University. His research interests include mentoring and linguistic development. Previous publications include sociological analyses of organisations and psychological approaches to social work.

Geraldine Oliver

Geraldine Oliver is a Senior Lecturer in Education/Early Years at the University of Teesside. She is the Programme Coordinator for Early Years at the University of Teesside and has developed academic modules as well as having taught extensively within Early Years. Her research interests include mentoring and linguistic development.

Lynn Trodd

Lyn Trodd is a Senior Lecturer in the School of Education at Hertfordshire. She has run the Phase 1 pilot for EYPS and is involved in teaching the National Professional Qualification in Integrated Centre Leadership, and the Sector-Endorsed Foundation Degrees in Playwork and in Early Years.

Gill Goodliff

Gill Goodliff is a Lecturer in Early Years at the Open University where she teaches on work-based learning courses in the Sector-Endorsed Foundation Degree in Early Years and is a Lead Assessor for Early Years Professional Status. Her professional background with young children and their families was predominantly in the Public Voluntary and Independent sector. Her current research focuses on the professional development and identities of Early Years practitioners and young children's spirituality.

Acknowledgements

Thanks go to colleagues and students at the University of Teesside and partner colleges for their contribution to the debates and discussions that have helped to form this book. Thanks also go to Professors John Fulton of Surrey University and John Davis of All Souls College, Oxford for encouraging perseverance in reconciling studying, research, writing, teaching and administrating.

The authors thank the staff at Learning Matters, particularly Julia Morris, and Jennifer Clark for their patience, developmental comments and efficiency. Lyn Trodd and Gill Goodliff are also to be thanked for their guidance and collegiate support.

As ever I am particularly grateful for the support of my parents and my wife Karen and children Bernadette, Teresa and Michael. Without them tomorrow would always be a much harder day.

Dr Ewan Ingleby, June 2008

Foreword from the series editors

This book is one of a series which will be of interest to all those following pathways towards achieving Early Years Professional Status (EYPS). This includes students on Sector-Endorsed Early Years Foundation Degree programmes and undergraduate Early Childhood Studies degree courses as these awards are key routes towards EYPS.

The graduate EYP role was developed as a key strategy in government commitment to improve the quality of Early Years care and education in England, especially in the private, voluntary and independent sectors. Policy documents and legislation such as *'Every Child Matters: Change for Children'* DfES (2004); the *'Ten Year Childcare Strategy: Choice for Parents - the Best Start for Children'* HMT (2004), and the Childcare Act, 2006, identified the need for high-quality, well-trained and educated professionals to work with the youngest children. At the time of writing (July 2008), the Government's aim is to have Early Years Professionals (EYPs) in all Children's Centres by 2010 and in every full day care setting by 2015.

In *Applied Social Science for Early Years* Ewan Ingleby and Geraldine Oliver draw on their experiences of teaching Early Years practitioners to provide a text which contextualises the required knowledge and understanding of an EYP in an accessible, relevant way. The book makes links to the National Standards for Early Years Professional Status. It also provides useful case studies that illustrate the application of social science theory in the work of an Early Years Professional and self-assessment questions (with suggested answers) to support readers' confidence in their own understanding.

This book is distinctive in the series because it provides some of the essential underpinning knowledge needed by candidates who wish to achieve EYP Status. It aims to deepen the understanding of its readers so that they become more aware of why they work in certain ways as a practitioner. In this way it aims to support reflection on practice and to help EYPs to articulate their thinking when they seek to influence other practitioners in their roles as change agents and leaders of practice.

Applied Social Science for Early Years will support candidates on any of the pathways towards achieving Early Years Professional Status and we are delighted to commend it to you.

Lyn Trodd · · · · · · · · Gill Goodliff
University of Hertfordshire · · · The Open University
July 2008

Introduction

This book applies social science subjects such as psychology, sociology, social policy and research methods to Early Years. These subjects inform much of the academic curriculum within many Early Years programmes. They are subjects that make an especially important contribution to understanding children's growth and development. Applying social science to Early Years can help to raise standards and ensure good practice. This aim is as relevant today as it ever has been. Clark and Waller (2007, p168) draw attention to the 'persistent division' between care and education and the need for strategies to coordinate these services. Doyle (2005, p13) comments that this situation can lead to the loss of centrality of the rights of the child especially when the emphasis is placed upon 'policy and procedure' at the expense of recognising children's needs.

This is one of the reasons why this book discusses the application of social science to Early Years. All of the social science subjects are important to Early Years, because they offer explanations of complex aspects of children's behaviour and development. The current Standards for Early Years Professionals are linked to applying social science to practice. These standards can be put into effect upon considering how social science subjects can be applied in working with children and families who have many differing needs. My own realisation of this important point occurred when working with children with mental health needs and learning disabilities within residential social work. I had previously studied academic social science and enjoyed interpreting aspects of my own personality and circumstances in relation to psychological and sociological theories. This interest was put into perspective upon experiencing the ways in which children's behaviour can be influenced through the application of psychological therapies. On reflection, the experience of care planning through applying psychological and sociological therapies to particular children was one of the most satisfying aspects of Early Years work. It is a memory that will always stay with me. A major aim of the book is to reveal that applying social science to Early Years can make professional practice much more effective. This application to practice can become a means whereby a balance is offered between what is intrapersonal and particular to individual practitioners alongside what is interpersonal and accepted as being general good practice between practitioners. This means that reflecting on how psychology, sociology, social policy and research methods inform practice is especially important within this book. It is a central theme that runs through each of the main chapters.

Standards for Early Years Professionals

Early Years professional practice is now informed by the Standards for Early Years Professionals. These standards emphasise the importance of professional training for Early Years staff so that children's needs can be met as fully as possible. This book aims to identify and analyse ways of applying social science to Early Years in relation to the Standards for Early Years professionals. These standards reveal the importance of working effectively within Early Years in order to raise life opportunities. Six key aspects of practice are identified by the standards.

- effective practice;

- communicating and working in partnership with families and carers;

- professional development.

Book structure

This book concentrates on applying social science to Early Years practice. There are formative activities that attempt to develop cognitive skills so that as well as identifying how social science can be applied to practice, there is academic analysis alongside synthesis in relation to one's own experience in Early Years.

An important theme of the book is to emphasise the importance of practitioners viewing social science in relation to practice. This means that the theoretical concepts are considered to be most useful when they are applied to particular Early Years issues. This is why all of the chapters in the book contain activities that aim to apply social science to particular Early Years contexts. These activities attempt to engage the reader with the idea that social science ought not to be thought of in isolation from practical contexts.

The book's chapters focus upon six main themes. The first chapter outlines some of the key psychological perspectives that are important for Early Years. There is an overview of behaviourism, humanism, psychodynamic, cognitive and biological perspectives. From the beginning of the book there is exemplification in order to show the therapies that are available for Early Years practitioners. As well as identifying the important ideas of each of the perspectives, there is analysis of the strengths and weaknesses of each of the perspectives as well as a critical appraisal of the effectiveness of the therapies that have their basis in each of the perspectives. These psychological perspectives are appraised in relation to a range of Early Years roles and contexts.

McGillivray (2007, p41) acknowledges that the Childcare Act 2006 now legislates for local authorities to work together to meet the needs of children and families. This legislation may be seen as a formal recognition of social responsibility. Chapter 2 considers this theme in explaining the importance of sociology for Early Years. The chapter explores the debate existing between perspectives such as functionalism and interactionism in relation to their lesser or greater acknowledgement of the importance of 'society'. The chapter applies the ideas of these perspectives in accounting for positive and negative social characteristics. This leads to an appraisal of how these two highly influential sociological perspectives may be applied to the Early Years context in explaining differing forms of social expression and in offering strategies to counter negative forms of social behaviour.

Chapter 3 focuses upon recent initiatives within social policy that have placed child rights at the centre of statutory legislation. The chapter discusses how and why particular policy directions have been formed. Explanation is offered for how and why particular policy directions have evolved with discussion of the subsequent impact of contemporary policy initiatives for children, families and Early Years workers.

Chapter 4 discusses the importance of language and literacy in early childhood. The chapter explores children's language acquisition in relation to the development of learning. The chapter also considers particular case-studies such as children with sensory impairments, learning disabilities, and language development deficits.

All of the main chapters within the book are designed to focus upon key areas of Early Years practice. Chapter 5 discusses the experience of different childhoods within the UK and within the international context. Handley (2005, p5) warns against 'seeing children as objects of processes rather than subjects'. This chapter adopts this idea by developing the theme that effective Early Years practice necessitates being aware of the variety of experiences that help to shape children over time and space. Within the UK and beyond there exists an enormous range of experiences of childhood and these experiences make an equally significant contribution to the interaction occurring between children and Early Years workers.

Chapter 6 identifies key research perspectives and key research methods that are used within early years. The chapter begins by identifying the research process. It then discusses the origins of key research paradigms such as normative, interpretive, and action research perspectives. The chapter considers key methodological strategies employed by qualitative and quantitative research in relation to Early Years. The chapter ends by discussing the relative merits of research paradigms and methods.

The book attempts to provide a comprehensive coverage of key themes impacting on Early Years practice. As opposed to being a general social science textbook it is specifically written for the Early Childhood Studies degree programme and attempts to combine practical experience alongside sound academic analysis.

Learning features

The book attempts to stimulate learning through interactive activities within each chapter. As well as these activities there are case-studies and research tasks. The book aims to develop analytical skills through a creative engagement with the content. Alongside the interactive learning activities there are supporting references so that you can synthesise knowledge of social science in relation to Early Years.

Professional development and reflective practice

A major aim of the Early Childhood Studies programme at the University of Teesside is to nurture professionals who are able to reflect on aspects of best practice. This book attempts to facilitate self-analysis in relation to social science and Early Years. From this self-reflection there is the possibility of development in relation to meeting the complex needs of children and families. If this aim is realised it will help to achieve some of the aims of the current Standards for Early Years Professionals.

REFERENCES

Clark, M. and Waller, T. (2007) *Early childhood education and care: policy and practice.* London: Sage.

Doyle, C. (2005) Protecting children, in Waller, T. (2005) *Early childhood: a multidisciplinary approach.* London: Paul Chapman.

Handley, G. (2005) Children's rights to participation, in Waller, T. (2005) *Early childhood: a multidisciplinary approach.* London: Paul Chapman.

McGillivray, G. (2007) Policy and practice in England, in Clark M, and Waller, T, (2007) *Early childhood education and care: policy and practice.* London: Sage.

1   Knowledge and understanding of psychology for EYPS

CHAPTER OBJECTIVES

After reading this chapter you should be able to:
- analyse some of the ways that psychology can be used by Early Years practitioners.

The chapter develops your knowledge and understanding of selected psychological theories accounting for children's growth and development. The material corresponds to 'S7', 'S14' and 'S23'in particular because of the focus on how an increased awareness of applied psychology enables children to achieve their full potential.

Introduction

This opening chapter introduces you to the discipline of psychology and discusses how psychology can be applied to Early Years in order to improve practice. Each school of psychology has a different understanding of what constitutes the self. This understanding is outlined, analysed and critically appraised in order to explore how psychology can be applied to Early Years. Throughout the chapter there are formative activities that reinforce learning in relation to the main psychological paradigms (or models) that are of relevance for Early Years practitioners.

Defining the discipline of psychology

REFLECTIVE TASK

What is your understanding of the word psychology?

Psychology is an academic discipline that studies a vast range of human and animal behaviour. Psychologists are not mind readers and they do not necessarily have access to our thoughts. They do not work solely with people who are mentally ill or people who are emotionally disturbed. These are common delusions and misinterpretations of the discipline.

'Psychology' is not as easy to define as it might initially appear. It is more than just a word. To a layperson an immediate reaction may be to associate psychology with 'reading peoples' minds' or 'analysing aspects of human behaviour'. A dictionary definition of psychology may give a precise explanation but this precision can disguise the complexity of the subject. An example of a dictionary definition is that psychology can be understood as being:

> *the scientific study of all forms of human and animal behaviour.*
>
> *(Online dictionary)*

Psychology is relevant for Early Years practitioners because it gives explanations for children's growth and development. This means that studying psychology enables you to increase your knowledge of key factors influencing children and families.

Origins of psychology

The word psychology is derived from two Greek words 'psyche', meaning mind and 'logos' meaning study so a literal translation is 'the study of the mind'. This means that psychology literally translates as the study of the mind. Malim and Birch (1998, p3) claim that the discipline began in 1879 when Wilhelm Wundt opened the first psychology laboratory at the University of Leipzig in Germany. Wundt focused upon 'introspection', meaning observing and analysing the structure of conscious mental processes. It was the emphasis placed upon measurement and control of thinking processes that marked the separation of psychology from its parent discipline philosophy.

The rise of behaviourism

Malim and Birch (1998, p8) argue that by 1920 the usefulness of this method was questioned. John B. Watson was one of a number of theorists who believed that it was wrong to focus upon introspection because this approach to studying psychology is immeasurable and so it invalidated its scientific credentials. Consequently Watson dedicated himself to the study of what has become known as 'behaviourism', or human behaviour that is measurable and observable. Behaviourism remained the dominant force in psychology over the next 30 years, especially in the USA. The emphasis was placed upon identifying the external factors that produce changes in behaviour, learning or conditioning using a stimulus response model.

Competing perspectives

As with many philosophical and sociological perspectives, psychology is characterised by competing paradigms or models of thought, with theorists becoming grouped together according to which perspective they adopt. Malim and Birch (1998, p9) argue that an interesting reaction to behaviourism came in the form of the Gestalt school of psychology emerging in Austria and Germany in the 1920s popularised by psychologists such as Wolfgang Kohler (1927). This branch of psychology takes a holistic approach considering that the whole person is greater and more complex than his or her individual characteristics and that this in turn complicates a focus upon the external factors producing thoughts and behaviour.

Psychodynamic psychology

A further criticism of behaviourism developed through the twentieth century as a result of the legacy of Sigmund Freud, possibly the most famous psychologist of all. Malim and Birch (1998, p9) argue that Freud proposes that the mind is a combination of conscious and unconscious thoughts. If we accept that this is the case, Freud's theory can be used to challenge behaviourism because it implies that human thought and behaviour is more complex than the behaviourist notion that external variables cause thought and behaviour.

Cognitive psychology

Alongside psychodynamic theory there emerged a further significant theory that places the emphasis upon thinking processes or cognition, in other words the ways in which we attain, retain and regain information. Within cognitive psychology an emphasis is placed on identifying what happens within the mind after a stimulus has been received. The mind is seen as being like an information-processor, almost akin to a computer. Malim and Birch (1998, p25) explain this perspective by arguing that 'human beings are seen as information processors who absorb information from the outside world, code and interpret it, store and retrieve it'.

Biological psychology

This view is reinforced by some of the current developments within psychology. The scientific advances of the 1990s and beyond in relation to identifying the genetic and hormonal composition of the human mind have generated enormous interest in the idea that thoughts and behaviour are determined by our biology. This may be considered to be a reductionist argument because it reduces complex thoughts and behaviour to a few variables such as hormones and genes. The ideas within biological psychology may prove to be yet another passing paradigm contributing to the on-going dialogue about the discipline of psychology that in turn will be criticised and revised.

From this initial discussion about what is meant by the word psychology we can ask a further question in relation to the nature of the human mind.

Is the human mind is the same as the human brain?

Do you think that the mind is the same as the brain? List your reasons to support this view. Write down the reasons to support a different view that someone might give.

One answer to this question is that there is no definite answer. Philosophers have speculated for hundreds, perhaps thousands, of years about what has come to be known as 'the mind-brain problem'. Whether you focus upon the mind or the brain depends upon your fundamental understanding of how psychology should be studied. Many psychological perspectives such as behaviourism, humanism, psychodynamic and cognitive theories emphasise the importance of the mind. This is because each of these perspectives has a clear understanding or model of the mind. In contrast biological perspectives are more likely to place an emphasis upon the genes and hormones influencing the brain.

We can now look at exploring some of the psychological perspectives. This is a way of adding detail to our introductory explanations of what the subject area of psychology is. It is also a means of setting the scene before we look at how psychology can be applied to Early Years practice and the role of the Early Years Professional in particular.

The schools of psychology

In the following table there is a summary of five major schools of psychology together with a brief description of their key features.

These schools of thought are especially useful to you as an EYP because of the influence they have had in shaping the academic concerns of psychology which underpin your work with children. An an EYP you will need to influence the practice of the practitioners by convincing them through modelling and discussion. Knowledge and understanding of the competing perspectives in psychology will help you. The origins of the schools of thought go back to some of the earliest philosophical ideas to have influenced western thought. The proposition that there are forces beyond the individual that shape social reality goes back to the ideas of the Greek philosopher Plato. This idea is central to behaviourism so the perspective has its intellectual origins in this classical thought. The notion that individuals interpret their social world as opposed to being ultimately shaped by this world goes back to the ideas of Aristotle (Audi, 1995). This philosophy is of central importance to humanism. In other words the genesis of the perspective's dominant idea

Table 1.1 Schools of psychology

School	Key features
Behaviourism	Human behaviour is seen as being shaped by environmental forces and is a collection of learned responses to external stimuli. The key learning process is known as 'conditioning'.
Humanism	The individual is seen as being unique, rational and self-determining. Present experience is held to be as important as past experience.
Psychodynamic theory	The mind is seen as being a combination of conscious thoughts and the workings of the unconscious mind. The unconscious mind expresses itself through dreams and behaviour we are not consciously aware of.
Cognitive theory	This perspective looks at what happens after a stimulus but before a response. The human mind is likened to a computer. People are seen as information processors, selecting, coding, storing and retrieving information when needed.
Neurobiological theory	Behaviour is considered as being determined by genetic, physiological and neurobiological factors and processes.

can be traced back to these early times. A summary of each of the key perspectives developing the definitions given in Table 1.1 follows. A definition of each of the key perspectives is given. Key figures influencing the perspective are identified and central terms within each perspective are explained.

Behaviourism

Behaviourists emphasise the importance of external factors in producing thoughts within the human mind. A key behaviourist idea is that every individual enters the world as a 'clean slate'. The surrounding environment is considered to be the 'chalk' etching its marks upon the 'slate' of the mind. This means that the individual enters the world without a fixed identity and that social factors are responsible for making the individual whosoever s/he becomes. The Jesuit notion of 'giving me the boy and I'll show you the man' equates to this idea. This suggests that we become who we are as a result of factors beyond and outside individuals.

A number of psychologists have become famous members of the behaviourist school of thought. Burrhus Skinner, Edward Thorndike, John Watson and Ivan Pavlov have become synonymous with behaviourist psychology. All of these psychologists share in common the belief that external factors are of critical importance in producing thoughts and behaviour.

The terms 'classical conditioning' and 'operant conditioning' are particularly important within behaviourism. Classical conditioning is associated with the work of Ivan Pavlov. It has become associated with the ways whereby biological responses are regulated by external factors. This produces what has become phrased as a 'conditioned response' where a form of behaviour occurs in association with a particular stimulus. Operant conditioning is a term that has become associated with the work of Burrhus Skinner. It refers to the link that exists between positively affirming behaviour that reinforces a particular stimulus. To give a simple example, if a child responds favourably to a parental instruction the child is usually praised. This reinforcement of learning through praise is therefore a type of operant conditioning. In the following case study there is the exemplification of when children may experience classical and operant conditioning.

CASE STUDY

Sophie is four years old and she has just started school. She has been in the school for one month and she has already learned many of the school rules. She has noticed that when the school bell rings at 9 am she has to line-up with all the other children and stand still with her arms by her side looking out for her class teacher Mrs Black. At first a number of the infants did not know what to do when the bell rang at the start of the school day. The sight of all the other children moving into line upset some of the infants as they felt afraid and anxious because they did not know what they were supposed to do. This association of the bell ringing and anxiety has gradually made the infants copy what the other children were doing. Today when the bell rang at 9 am nearly all of the infants copied the other older children so that they would not stand out and feel anxious. They got into line standing with their arms by their sides looking out for Mrs Black. They moved a little bit more than the other older children but their response to the bell ringing at 9 am has become conditioned into acceptable behaviour. On Friday Sophie received a 'star badge' for her good work. She felt very pleased as she had to go onto the stage at assembly and receive her gold badge. Sophie remembered her parents' words that in school she should always try her hardest.

Humanism

Humanism does acknowledge the importance of environmental factors on the mind but it places an emphasis upon the individual interpretation of external factors. This means that as opposed to emphasising the importance of external variables, attention is given to the importance of individuals interpreting social reality. Humanism can be associated with the philosophy of Immanuel Kant and his 'Copernican revolution' of thought (Audi, 1995, p400). As opposed to asking about the reality of the universe, Kant changes the focus of the argument to ask about how individuals understand social reality. Humanism asks a similar question. As opposed to focusing upon how external variables produce thoughts, the humanist emphasis is on how individuals make sense of external variables.

Humanism has become associated with the work of Carl Rogers and Abraham Maslow. Maslow proposes that all humans have a 'hierarchy of needs' and that individual thoughts are influenced by the extent to which these physiological and intellectual needs are being met. Carl Rogers has had a particularly important influence on humanism and it may be claimed that Rogers is the founding father of psychological humanism. His work is also influential in what is considered as being effective Early Years practice. One of the most important Rogerian ideas to have influenced social care is the proposal that anxiety is a product of what has become termed as a 'would/should dilemma'. This means that an individual wants to do something but they are unable to achieve this wish. According to Rogers this then generates tension within the individual that in turn produces anxiety.

In applying therapy to resolve the would/should dilemma, Rogers recommends that the therapist must have a congruent or genuine interest in the person. This means that empathy is a central concept to the Rogerian model of client centred therapy. The ideal aim is to lead the person being counselled to their 'inner beautiful self' so that the individual's would/should dilemma can be overcome.

REFLECTIVE TASK

Think about your own personal development. To what extent do you think that your personality has been formed as a result of external environmental factors? To what extent do you think that your personality is a product of your unique personality?

FEEDBACK

Most people would probably accept that their personality is a combination of external environmental variables alongside their own unique personal traits. In other words the person is a product of factors that are both outside and inside the individual. It is interesting, however, to consider why and when the emphasis placed upon the individual and the environment varies. In this country particular social, economic and religious variables have influenced the extent to which one's surroundings or one's personality are held accountable for personality development. In the UK there are many communities that emphasise self-responsibility. If one claims that the environment is responsible for personal development this may be regarded as an attempt to disown one's accountability for individual life circumstances. Some of the popular movements of the 1960s and 1970s may have changed this perception but the prevailing thought in the UK today would seem to be that individual characteristics are especially important in determining one's personality. This may lessen the importance of the behaviourist perspective and make humanism a more influential explanation of individual circumstances.

Psychodynamic theory

Psychodynamic psychology is associated with the ideas of one of the most famous psychologists, Sigmund Freud. Freud's theory postulates that thoughts are a product of the working of both the conscious and the unconscious mind (Gross, 1999, p969). We have conscious thoughts that we are aware of and unconscious thoughts that appear in our mind in the form of dreams. Moreover, what happens in our conscious mind in turn influences what thoughts filter through to our unconscious mind.

Freud considers that there are three especially important components to every individual (Gross, 1999, p591). There is the 'id' or biological physiology of maleness and femaleness. There is the 'ego' or social self to regulate our biological 'id'. There is also the 'superego' existing beyond the individual that generates a common understanding of our social identity.

Freud claims that all individuals go through a number of stages of development. From 0–1 a child is considered to be in an oral stage of development. This means that the infant is preoccupied with its mouth. This then leads to the anal stage of development from 1–2 when the infant becomes aware of its capacity to excrete and urinate. The next developmental stage is the phallic stage of development when boys and girls become increasingly aware of biological maleness and femaleness. Freud claims that this occurs between the ages of 3–6 resulting in a close relationship between a boy and his mother and a girl and her father. After the phallic stage of development there is what Freud terms as a latent phase of development. This occurs between the ages of 6–12 as the individual becomes more concerned with their social identity as they become increasingly aware of their ego state. The theory states that the final stage of development is the genital stage from the age of 12 onwards when Freud proposes that males and females become increasingly aware of their adult reproductive capabilities.

Freud's theory introduces the idea that human beings hold the potential for fixated behaviour. This means that an individual could become negatively confined to a particular stage (or stages) of development. As an example, if an infant experienced the trauma of losing its mother at the age of 1, there is the possibility of this individual developing what Freud terms an 'oral fixation'. This fixated behaviour expresses itself at a later age through consciously chosen behaviour exemplified by the oral fixation of alcoholism. What makes the theory so original is that it is claimed that the conscious choice of behaviour has its origins in the depths of the unconscious mind. Proponents of the theory claim that this repression can be released through psychodynamic counselling. This counselling may be needed in a situation when the individual has experienced a physical and/or emotional crisis during their development.

Crises leading to fixated behaviour can occur at any stage of development. According to Freud this personal development directs the individual in the direction of one of two forces, either towards 'Thanatos' or 'Eros'. Eros, the Greek god of love is interpreted by Freudians as contributing to an individual's optimism. Thanatos, the Greek personification of death is perceived as contributing to an individual's sense of pessimism. How one develops determines whether one's conscious frame of mind directs the individual to the good or otherwise. It can be argued that Freud's legacy is to have left one of the most influential psychological theories to contribute to the discipline. It is however important to recognise that just because the theory is famous does not mean it is correct. This point will be developed later in the chapter.

Cognitive theory

Cognitive psychology can be understood as being a branch of psychology that is interested in what happens after a stimulus but before a response. It is a school of psychology that has become associated with the work of Jean Piaget and Lev Vygotsky.

Malim and Birch (1998, p27) argue that Piaget is 'the most significant figure in the study of cognitive development'. Piaget's model of cognitive development has become particularly influential within psychology. According to Piaget the human mind develops over time as an individual is stimulated by its surroundings. From the ages of 0–2 the child has basic thoughts or 'schemata'. Piaget claims that these initial thoughts are limited and instinctive. A baby has a 'crying schema', a 'grasping schema' and a 'feeding schema'. These thought processes develop from the age of 2 as the infant becomes capable of speech and develops what Piaget phrases as 'symbolic thought'. It is also proposed that between the ages of 2–7 the child's problem solving skills are limited because of two terms Piaget phrases as 'centration' and 'egocentricism'. By 'centration' Piaget means that the child can see one aspect of a situation's reality but not the total picture. As an example, a child between the ages of 2–7 may think that a ton of lead is heavier than a ton of feathers because they 'centrate' or focus on one aspect of the problem. The child assumes that lead is a metal and therefore heavier than 'fluffy' feathers. This means that the child may not see that in fact both quantities are the same weight. By 'egocentrism' Piaget means that a child cannot see the true nature of a problem because problem solving occurs in relation to what the child knows about reality. As an example, if a child aged 2–7 is asked what noise a reindeer makes they may say 'clip clop' instead of 'I don't know'. This is due to egocentrism. The child thinks that the reindeer looks like a horse and knows that a horse makes a 'clip clop' sound so it assumes that reindeer also make a 'clip clop' sound. Piaget claims that in order to progress through this stage of development the child needs to interact with its environment through play.

As a consequence of linguistic development the infant becomes capable of more complex thought so that by the age of 7 the preoperational stage has ended and the child is able to complete complex problem solving. This stage of development is phrased 'concrete operations'. This is because Piaget claims that children aged between 7–11 need to use props if they are to complete problem solving activities. From 7–11 a child can calculate that 3 apples + 2 apples add up to make 5 apples but Piaget claims that the child needs to have the actual apples to hand in order to complete the calculation. As this interaction occurs the child will develop what Piaget phrases as 'reversible thinking'. This is the final stage of cognitive development occurring around 11 years of age. Once reversible thought has been reached it is possible to problem solve within the mind, without using the props that a 7 year old child needs. When one can apply reversible thinking to solving a problem, it means that one can see within one's mind that 3+2 is the same as 7-2.

Lev Vygotsky's work is seen as complementing Piaget's theory as opposed to being a radically different cognitive perspective (Malim and Birch, 1998, p469). Vygotsky places more emphasis upon the social factors influencing the child's cognitive development. One of Vygotsky's central ideas is the notion of each individual having a 'scaffold' of persons aiding their cognitive development. According to the nature of the scaffold, the child's cognitive development is affected in either negative or positive ways. If for example the child's peers are interested in academic issues, this social scaffold will impact upon cognitive development and make the child more academic. If the opposite situation occurs it leads to negative cognitive development. It can be argued that this theory complements Piaget's work because it explains why some children are 'late developers' and reach the stage of reversible thought beyond the age of 11. Vygotsky uses the term 'ZPD' or 'Zone of Proximal Development' to refer to when an individual has fulfilled their cognitive potential. This stage of development may occur at 11. It may occur beyond the age of 11. What becomes critical is the influence of one's cognitive development in relation to the 'scaffold' of individuals influencing one's cognitive development.

Biological psychology

It can be argued that biological psychology is becoming of increasing importance due to the recent scientific advances in understanding human genetics. The biological perspective places an emphasis on the link between the thoughts of individuals and their hormonal and chromosomal composition. It is accepted by the scientific community that males and females differ in one pair of chromosomes and that before the infant is born the presence of a 'Y' chromosome leads to the development of testes. This in turn leads to the production of the hormone testosterone. As a consequence males produce more androgens whereas females produce oestrogen and progesterone. Biologists such as Milton Diamond (1980) and Roger Gorski (1966) emphasise the importance of biology in producing thoughts. It has been discovered that the male brain is physically different from the female brain due to the influence of the hormone testosterone. According to this theory the inevitable consequence is that the thoughts occurring within the mind must have some biological basis and that differences in thought patterns are crucially linked to hormonal and chromosomal factors.

Applying psychology to Early Years

All of the psychological perspectives that have been introduced within this chapter can be applied to Early Years practice and the role of the Early Years Professional. There are a number of psychological therapies and each one has the potential to improve and enhance professional practice. Moreover if the therapies are combined they offer the potential to give holistic therapy in order to assist children with complex needs. This next section of the chapter introduces some of the therapies that could be used by Early Years Professionals. This is one example of how psychology can be applied to the Early Years context.

Behaviourist therapies

One of the most well-known behaviourist therapies is called 'token economy'. The therapy is based on the principle of conditioning responses, effectively manipulating choice so that positive behaviour occurs. Most children have complex thoughts and they are likely to choose whether to conform with or rebel against accepted social requirements. This acceptance or rebellion can be overt and explicit or implicit and assumed. Token economy attempts to produce conformity of response. At the end of every day in which the individual has complied with what is required a reward or 'token' is offered. This token has to have appeal and value to the person receiving the therapy. If there is a lack of compliance with the programme the token is denied. After a short period of time, for example five days of compliance, the recipient is rewarded with a bigger treat or prize. Token economy is used within many nurseries and primary schools. It is a behaviourist attempt to get children to comply with what is required of them within the school environment. It is a therapy that is also used within other Early Years contexts, but as we shall see later in the chapter, it is a therapy that is not without its critics.

Another therapy that is available for Early Years practitioners is biofeedback. This therapy may be used with children who have been referred for professional help because they are highly anxious. Music, light, aroma and relaxing furnishings are combined to produce an environment that can physically relax the individual. The therapy is essentially attempting to produce relaxing thoughts within the child's mind by manipulating external variables.

A third popular therapy that has its origins within behaviourist theory is known as 'systematic desensitisation'. This therapy may be used with children who have phobias. The child is made to come to terms with his/her phobia in a controlled environment. It is proposed that as a result of gradually exposing the child to the phobia in a non-threatening way, the phobic object becomes manageable and increasingly less debilitating. Once again the emphasis is placed upon the importance of the practitioner manipulating the child's thoughts in order to produce positive ways of thinking about the phobia. The following case study example outlines the ways in which behaviourism can be applied to Early Years. It also reveals some of the potential difficulties that exist when particular therapies are applied to children with particular needs.

CASE STUDY

Peter lives in residential care. He is 7 and has learning disabilities but there has been no definitive diagnosis of the nature of his disability. He is thought to have a combination of autism and learning disability. Before Peter goes to sleep at night he has a habit of getting all of his shoes from his wardrobe and throwing them down the stairs. In an attempt to get Peter to change his behaviour a token economy programme has been designed by the members of the multidisciplinary team who work with him. Peter loves watching cartoons on television and the token economy programme involves giving Peter a token on each day when he does not throw his shoes down the stairs. Peter likes chocolate and when he has complied with the care programme he is given a chocolate treat of his choice. If he does not follow what is expected of him Peter is denied this reward. Upon receiving five tokens, Peter is given the opportunity to watch a cartoon DVD of his choice. Some of the staff working with Peter have expressed concerns that there are ethical problems with this behaviour modification programme. There are concerns that this conditioning violates Peter's right to choose what he should and should not do.

Humanist therapies

The humanist philosophy of Carl Rogers is at the centre of what is deemed as being 'good practice' within Early Years work. Rogers proposes an egalitarian model of practice in which the practitioner is not aloof from the child but 'with' the child. Empathy is a particularly important aspect of the Rogerian way. The practitioner must be there for the child and prepared to be genuine and assertive. According to Rogers a genuine practitioner can enable children's growth and development.

Effective practice is facilitated upon resolving the 'would/should dilemma'. Rogers considers that this dilemma is the cause of anxiety that in turn prevents child development. Practitioners should also direct children to their 'beautiful inner self'. Rogers believes that all individuals are innately good and that it is only the tension that results from a would/should dilemma that makes the individual a less than good person. Through a genuine and empathetic relationship it is postulated that the would/should dilemma will be replaced by an assertive awareness of one's inner goodness. Although there are many applications for this type of therapy, the generalising assumptions that are made within humanism can mean that its application is restricted. This argument is exemplified in the following case study example and in the final section of the chapter.

CASE STUDY

Julie has recently qualified as a teaching assistant and she is working with children aged 7 to 8 in an inner city school. Within the last few months there has been an escalation of racial tension between black and white youths. The situation is further complicated by an outbreak of violence between Asian and Afro-Caribbean youths. As a student Julie was inspired by the ideas of Carl Rogers during a 'Promoting Positive Behaviour' module and she bases her teaching approach upon the principles of client-centred therapy. Within one of her first teaching sessions with a young Asian boy, Julie is devastated when the child runs out of the classroom when she is reading a story to the children. Julie realises that her values are very different from the values of this child and that this limits the application of client-centred therapy. In the past she has found that this therapy works with white children who seem to share many of her values but it is an altogether different challenge applying these ideas in this particular context.

Psychodynamic therapies

The psychodynamic model of the mind holds that conscious thoughts are influenced by the unconscious mind. This means that therapy involves releasing what is being unconsciously repressed. This then enables the individual to deal with these thoughts within the conscious mind. The psychodynamic therapist is responsible for interpreting what is within the individual's unconscious mind by analysing dreams and/or using hypnotherapy. Dream and fantasy analysis become a means of interpreting what is being repressed. It is considered to be imperative for unconscious thoughts to be released into the conscious mind in order to lessen the effects of repression. The Freudian model holds that fixated behaviour has its basis in repression so that the critical role of the therapist is one of releasing repressed thoughts and then recommending ways of consciously dealing with these thoughts.

The psychodynamic model is hierarchical as opposed to being equalitarian. The omniscient therapist is in a position of power over his/her clients a characteristic that can be deemed as being opposed to the equalitarian approach of Carl Rogers. This has consequences for the situations in which the therapy can be used and the clients upon whom the therapy should be used. This critique of psychodynamic therapy is exemplified in the subsequent case study.

CASE STUDY

Daniel is 6 and he has not attended school for over five months because he suffers from 'panic attacks'. He does not know why he experiences these panic attacks but he says that whenever he thinks about going to school he is unable to eat and that he has 'butterflies' in his stomach. Since there is no conscious explanation for his panic attacks, Daniel's psychiatrist has recommended a number of hypnotherapy sessions in order to identify if there is an unconscious reason for Daniel's behaviour. Under hypnosis Daniel talks about his anxieties about school, in particular his fear of some of the older pupils and of a recent incident when an older boy physically assaulted him in the school yard. Daniel had never disclosed this incident to anyone before and this was thought to be a major benefit of the hypnotherapy sessions. When Daniel was asked about this incident after his hypnotherapy had finished he said that this wasn't the main reason for his fear of school and that he still did not know why he was having his panic attacks. This was a difficulty of the hypnotherapy sessions. Although it did appear to shed light on some of the things that Daniel was repressing it still did not explain a reason for the panic attacks that both Daniel and his psychiatrist could unanimously agree upon. Daniel's psychiatrist said that he thought Daniel was having panic attacks because he was afraid of being bullied but Daniel denied this and said he didn't know what was causing the anxiety.

Cognitive therapies

Cognitive psychologists emphasise the importance of studying what happens after a stimulus but before a reaction. They are interested in the processes within the mind that produce thoughts, not in a biological sense but in terms of cognitive processes. It is proposed that through manipulating these cognitive processes one's thought processes can change. If, for example a child is unable to control their anger, it may be possible to apply cognitive therapy so that this anger is effectively managed. By counselling the individual to consciously change the thought processes occurring within the mind so that they think differently, there follows a cognitive restructuring. This allows the individual to think about the world in a different way. It is a therapy relying on psychological techniques as opposed to a medical therapy. If it is combined with other psychological therapies it can offer a potential solution to various psychological problems such as low self-esteem and inability to manage anger. The following case study example outlines how cognitive therapy can be applied to a particular example of anger management.

> ### CASE STUDY
>
> *Taylor is 5 and comes from a travelling family who have recently settled into the local community. He has a younger sister but his father has left the family home. Taylor is becoming prone to increasingly violent outbursts. It appears that he gradually becomes angry and then attacks his mother, his sister or both. Taylor's mother has become very concerned about these outbursts. In a recent incident Taylor screamed at his sister that he was going to 'strangle' her and Taylor's mother admitted that she was finding it hard to cope. The family have been helped by social services and Taylor's social worker referred the child to a cognitive behaviourist therapist who began to counsel Taylor. The therapy seemed to have some success when Taylor and his mother attended the sessions. It was explained to Taylor's mother that she must always maintain control of the situation when Taylor was having these outbursts by thinking in a non-aggressive and assertive way. When Taylor was having an aggressive outburst he had to be isolated from his mother and his sister. Taylor's mother was told that she should go and see Taylor at 5 minute intervals to ask if he had 'calmed down' so that Taylor would learn that a consistent strategy was in place to deal with his violent outbursts. The combination of anger management and applied behaviourism seemed to make a dramatic difference in controlling Taylor's violent outbursts.*

Biological therapies

Biological psychology attempts to understand the human mind by applying traditional western scientific principles. Therapies are based on the idea that thought processes are determined by the genetic and hormonal nature of the brain. It is also proposed that thought processes can be influenced by drug therapy. As an example, an overly aggressive child may be diagnosed as being overly aggressive because of the presence of too much testosterone within the body. This male hormone may need to be regulated by medication that lessens the aggressive impulses that are produced within the mind.

In the application of therapies based upon biological psychology, Early Years workers may be required to monitor the drug therapy of particular children. To give an example, it has been discovered that in some instances placing the individual on a drug regime based on dopamine can regulate schizophrenia. If levels of dopamine within the brain determine the presence or otherwise of schizophrenic tendencies it can be argued that drug therapies have their value within Early Years practice. It may also be argued that the precise link between the chemical composition of the brain and thought processes has never been exactly established and that this psychological perspective has not developed as yet to the extent that it can offer every possible solution for every possible psychological need.

> ### REFLECTIVE TASK
>
> *Think about each of the schools of psychology outlined in Table 1.1 and suggest how they might explain child obesity.*

Each of the psychological schools of thought would answer the question differently. Behaviourist psychologists think that the external environment shapes the individual. This means that obesity is considered to be a form of learned behaviour. The way to change the behaviour is through systems of reward and punishment that encourage healthy eating and discourage 'binge eating'. Humanists such as Carl Rogers would interpret obesity as being a sign of anxiety. Anxiety is a product of what Rogers describes as a 'would/should' dilemma, in other words an individual is not able to do what they would like to do. Resolve this dilemma and they are less likely to become obese. Psychoanalysts consider that conscious thoughts are influenced by what is within the unconscious mind. Obesity is considered to be a conscious fixation resulting from a repressed experience. It may be postulated that when the individual was a baby they had a traumatic experience during their oral stage of development and that the conscious act of 'binge eating' is a means of releasing this thought. The way to resolve this fixation is to have psychodynamic counselling whereby the counsellor can help the individual to resolve the conflict between unconscious and conscious thoughts. Neurobiological psychologists explain behaviour through analysing an individual's genetic composition. The implication is that obesity is a genetic disorder. The way to stop obese behaviour is to isolate and amend the biological gene promoting this behaviour. At present this procedure is talked about as opposed to being done. Cognitive psychologists would explain obesity as being part of an individual's cognitive map or thinking processes. It is a type of behaviour that comes from within the mind. In order to stop individuals 'binge eating' it may be proposed that the individual needs to have a cognitive restructuring of their thinking processes via cognitive counselling.

PRACTICAL TASK

When you are in an Early Years setting take a research diary and make a note of which therapies are being applied by the staff you meet. Analyse the effectiveness of the therapies by identifying which therapies work and why you think they are working. Make sure that you respect principles of confidentiality!

We can now complete our introductory chapter by focusing our discussion on critically appraising the psychological perspectives in terms of their value for Early Years.

Critical appraisal of how psychological therapies can be used in Early Years settings

There is no single perspective that holds all the answers to solving the problems faced by many children within Early Years settings. This means that the psychological therapies that have been outlined have limitations if they are applied in isolation.

Appraising behaviourism

The behaviourist therapies that have been summarised can make the mistake of focusing upon external variables to such an extent that the particular needs of individuals are not met. Every human being does not react in the same way to an external response. Even complex mammals such as dolphins can defy the laws of operant conditioning by doing the opposite to what they are expected to do. This means that there can be no scientific certainty of the therapies that are informed by this perspective. There is a further difficulty with behaviourist therapies that may be summarised as being linked to the unique nature of the human mind. There are profound ethical difficulties with therapies such as token economy. It can be claimed that token economy programmes do not respect dignity and human rights. A token economy programme is essentially saying 'do this for me and you will be rewarded'. This is a power relationship and it could be argued that the child is being manipulated in hierarchical non-egalitarian ways. This means that there are critiques of behaviourist therapies and concerns that they have limited application to Early Years. It leads Malim and Birch (1998, p24) to criticise behaviourist therapies because they can be 'mechanistic' and that they 'overlook the realm of consciousness and subjective experience'.

Appraising humanism

It can also be proposed that there are limitations in the application of Rogerian client-centred therapy. For the child to accept the importance of resolving the would/should dilemma it is important that they share similar values to the therapist. The child needs to accept that the values of the therapist are important so that there can be a situation where there is a link between what both therapist and child want to achieve. There are, however, many instances when the values of the child may be opposed to the values of the therapist. This can be exemplified within a school environment in which the pupils do not want to achieve what their teachers perceive as being important. This is supported by research that has been completed on the 'chav' subculture within the north-east of England. It is also acknowledged by Anne Watson (2004) in her discussion of the failings of the wider academic curriculum within the UK. Watson argues that it is not so much that the curriculum is a bad idea, it is more that there is little awareness of how to unite the values of the children and their teachers. This can mean that if an Early Years worker is to attempt using the ideas of Rogers the therapy cannot work because there is no common understanding of what is important and achievable. It is all very well to say that a would/should dilemma should be resolved but a child can only be directed to their 'inner beautiful self' if they perceive that self through a shared sense of identity with their therapist. Malim and Birch (1998, p803) develop this criticism by arguing that a critical limitation with humanist therapies relates to the assumption that 'self-actualisation' is a principal human motivation. Self-actualisation may motivate particular groups of individuals but it cannot be assumed to be a universal characteristic of every human being at every point in time.

Appraising psychodynamic theory

It may be argued that psychodynamic therapy has as many limitations as uses. The model is not based upon a sound methodology and many of the theoretical ideas can be challenged. It is a theory that is built upon assumptions of how the mind operates. If this is the case, it can be argued that any successes within psychodynamic theory are due to good fortune as much as anything else. A more significant critique of psychodynamic therapy is that it is a theory that is laden with negative value assumptions. The therapist is perceived to be in control of interpreting the child's problems. The classic image of the psychiatric couch can be applied to psychodynamic theory. This means that there is no equality of dialogue. As opposed to influencing the therapeutic process, the individual is effectively disempowered by a therapist who tells 'what should be done' in order to resolve 'fixated behaviour'. Malim and Birch (1998, p802) reinforce this criticism by emphasising that within psychoanalytical therapies there are problems of 'validation'. It may be suggested that within psychodynamic therapy the truth is invented as opposed to being truth in itself.

Appraising cognitive theory

The cognitive psychology of Jean Piaget can also be criticised. It is a theory that may have been mistranslated and turned into an unworkable model of the mind. Can it be accepted that the human brain moves through the stages that have become accepted as integral to Piaget's model? If not and if thoughts develop through more of a process than the movement through distinct stages of development, it means that the potential application of cognitive therapy is called into question. A further criticism is that although one can take apart a computer and identify the microchips making up its component parts, the human brain is altogether more complex. All sorts of factors that are not necessarily conscious inform cognitive processes. This may mean that a perspective that focuses upon what happens after a stimulus but before a response is dealing with part of the picture, but not the whole picture of human thought. A further criticism of cognitive therapy is that the child's problem behaviours or thoughts are always changed to those that the therapist sees as being acceptable. Malim and Birch (1998, p801) question whether it can always be the case that the therapist has the correct perspective on the world and that the child's cognitive outlook is in need of total change.

Appraising biological psychology

The biological therapies that are available to Early Years may be criticised because of what we do not know as opposed to what we do know. There is still much work that needs to be done in order to understand the hormonal and genetic composition of the brain. There is also a degree of uncertainty as to why some chemical treatments work with some individuals and yet the same treatments are less effective in another identical context. This anxiety can be combined with the concern existing over the side effects of drug-based therapy and the ethical implications this has for children. Taking a particular pill might make someone less aggressive but if the consequences are the docility exemplified in 'One Flew Over the Cuckoo's Nest' this effectively reduces the individual's life chances. There is also the critique that biological psychology is reductionist. It reduces the complex functioning of the brain to the relationship existing between genes, chromosomes and hormones. By concentrating the focus on this single area it can be argued that there is a possibility that other variables influencing human thought and behaviour are overlooked.

C H A P T E R   S U M M A R Y

In this opening chapter psychology has been likened to an 'academic ship of fools'. It is a complex discipline with competing views on how the subject ought to be studied. It is a diverse discipline with a range of identifiable 'sub-areas' of interest. There are a number of schools of psychology, each of which has adopted its own model of the person. The chapter has defined and explored five major perspectives that are of use to Early Years workers. Examples of specific therapies have been provided and there has been a critical appraisal of each of the therapies. It may be argued that the best way to apply psychology to Early Years is to combine the perspectives and their therapies in such a way that the complex needs of individuals are more likely to be met. If this is done, it produces an holistic approach to meeting individual needs. If these therapies are combined with other perspectives from health and counselling there is the further likelihood that our understanding of child development can be enhanced. It may be argued that this is the best way to apply psychology to Early Years.

Self-assessment questions

1. What are the five major schools of psychology?

2. How can Early Years workers apply the schools of psychology to help children and maximise their professional practice?

3. Give an example strength and weakness of each of the psychological schools of thought?

Moving on

This chapter has introduced the schools of psychological thought. Chapter 2 introduces you to a number of key sociological perspectives. Try to think of how psychology and sociology can be applied to Early Years in order to meet the needs of children and families.

REFERENCES

Audi, R. (1995) *The Cambridge dictionary of philosophy*. Cambridge: Cambridge University Press.

Diamond, M. (1980) *Sexual decisions*. London: Little Brown.

Gorski, R., McLean-Evans, H., and Whalen, R. (1966) *The brain and gonadal function*. California: University of California Press.

Gross, R. (1999) *Psychology: the science of mind and behaviour*, 2nd edition. London: Hodder and Stoughton.

Gross, R.D. (2001) *Psychology: the science of mind and behaviour*. London: Hodder Arnold.

Kesey, K. (1962) *One flew over the cuckoo's nest*. London: Picador.

Kohler, W. (1927) *The mentality of apes*. London: Kegan Paul.

Malim, T. and Birch, A. (1998) *Introductory psychology*. London: Palgrave Macmillan.

Online dictionary. Online: (www.dictionary.reference.com).

Watson, A. (2004) Reconfiguring the public sphere: implications for analyses of educational policy. *British Journal of Educational Studies*, 52(3): 228–248.

FURTHER READING

Gross, R.D. (2001), *Psychology: the science of mind and behaviour*. London: Hodder Arnold.
An excellent textbook in terms of depth of content and analysis but the material is not always related to Early Years contexts.

Malim, T. and Birch, A. (1998), *Introductory psychology*. London: Palgrave Macmillan.
An excellent textbook that is written in an accessible way and makes clear links to applying psychology to Early Years contexts.

2 Sociology and Early Years

CHAPTER OBJECTIVES

After reading this chapter you should be able to:
- analyse some of the ways that sociology can be used by Early Years practitioners.

The chapter develops your knowledge and understanding of sociology and how it can be applied to the Early Years context. The chapter content is especially relevant to 'S2', 'S3', 'S8', 'S29' and 'S38' because these standards require you to reflect on how child development is influenced by social factors. The chapter provides an introduction to sociology and explores how the discipline can be applied to Early Years. There are a number of sociological perspectives and each one has a particular understanding of how social factors influence individuals. This understanding is outlined, analysed and critically appraised within the chapter. The chapter adopts a similar structure to Chapter 1 as there are formative activities that reinforce learning in relation to the main sociological perspectives that are of relevance for Early Years practitioners.

Sociology is a discipline that attempts to explain the social world. In some respects it is similar to psychology as there have been a number of thinkers who have influenced the subject area over time. It is an important academic discipline for Early Years practitioners because it explains how social factors influence the development of children and families. This chapter explores some of the key perspectives within sociology. Before we look at the main sociological perspectives and discuss how Early Years practitioners can apply these ideas it is important to identify what the term 'sociology' means.

Defining sociology

The word 'sociology' can evoke a number of reactions. It is a discipline that is often associated with politics, especially left-wing politics, a legacy of the influence of Karl Marx. It may also be equated with analyses of human communities and the attempts that are made to make sense of these differing social groups. A dictionary definition of sociology is that it is:

the study of companionship.

Online dictionary

REFLECTIVE TASK

What do you think this dictionary definition means? Is it similar or different from your understanding of sociology? How is it similar? How does it differ?

FEEDBACK

This definition of sociology may explain the discipline's literal meaning. Sociologists such as Auguste Comte, Emile Durkheim, Max Weber and Karl Marx are interested in studying human communities in order to understand how they have formed, how they function and how they develop. The influential ideas of all of these sociologists rest at the centre of the main perspectives that influence the discipline. This means that we can use this dictionary definition as a starting point in attempting to understand what sociology is in order to deepen our understanding of the key perspectives that have influenced the subject.

If we develop this initial understanding of sociology we can say that sociologists are not necessarily left-wing political activists and that this is a common delusion and misinterpretation of the discipline.

The word sociology is derived from the Latin for 'associate' ('socius'). This means that the literal translation of sociology is 'the study of association or companionship'. Paul Taylor (2004, p1) argues that although this definition of the subject is 'limited' it still identifies the main concern of the subject. This develops the argument of the American social scientist C. Wright Mills (1970) that if we are to understand individual experiences we have to look beyond the personal circumstances in which they occur. This idea implies that personal circumstances can only be understood if they are placed within a broader context of public factors. Taylor (2004, p2) also argues that the first wisdom of sociology is to make us realise that 'things are not what they seem'. The social world is made of a number of layers of meaning so this necessitates challenging the assumptions that may be made about the social world. It leads Peter Berger (1966) to argue that sociology is characterised by a particular way of thinking that is reluctant to accept obvious explanations of the social world. The result is a sceptical attitude to what is viewed as being 'common-sense'. Taylor (2004, p3) refers to Nietzsche's notion of the 'art of mistrust' to summarise this prevalent characteristic of sociology.

As well as the stereotypical notion that sociology is 'left-wing and political' there may also be an assumption that sociologists write about the obvious in an oblique way. Durkheim's (1952) work on 'suicide' may be developed to argue that generating a sense of 'community' and 'belonging' is important in reducing suicide. Critics of this finding may argue that this is an obvious point that does not have to be presented in an academic way.

Think about the above argument. Do you think that sociology is 'common sense written about in an oblique way'? If so why, or if not why not?

It is important to ensure that you are as open-minded as possible about any academic discipline so that you do not follow the stereotypical assumptions that can be made about certain subjects. Since sociology has become associated with challenging social assumptions it has also become equated with radical thought that is not always within the boundaries of conventional social thinking. This can mean that sociologists are regarded as being opposed to the established order. This potentially unsettling challenge can mean that sociologists are labelled in a negative way. This can be one of the reasons why the subject is criticised and derided. It is worth remembering that sociology has an enormous philosophical heritage that reformulates the ideas of Plato, Hegel, Kant and Heidegger. It may be wiser to digest the arguments of the main thinkers within sociology before assuming that the subject is characterised by 'common sense written about in an oblique way'.

We can now look at exploring some of these understandings of sociology. This adds layers of meaning to the initial explanations of how the discipline can be understood in relation to Early Years. Key perspectives informing the discipline will be introduced before we analyse how sociology can be applied to Early Years.

The sociological perspectives

In the following table there is a summary of three highly influential sociological perspectives with a brief description of their key features.

These perspectives are especially important because of the influence they have had in shaping the academic concerns of sociology. Marshall (1994) argues that the ideas within the perspectives have been informed by the philosophy of Plato, Hegel, Kant and Heidegger. The Durkheimian focus upon the idea that society is greater than the individual links to the philosophy of Plato. This is because Plato has popularised the idea of the existence of an intelligence that is above and beyond the individuals within society (Audi, 1995, p618). The opposite idea that individuals are consciously creative so that they shape the social world links to the philosophy of Kant (Marshall, 1994, p265). It is also central to Husserl's interpretative philosophy that is in turn associated with Heidegger's focus on the importance of individual experiences (Marshall, 1994, p213). It can also be argued that an important characteristic of conflict theory is to view social processes as being opposed to each other in a way that is similar to what has been popularised as the Hegelian notion of 'thesis, antithesis and synthesis' (Audi, 1995, p315). This means that the perspectives can

Table 2.1 Sociological perspectives

School	Key features
Functionalism	Social behaviour is a product of 'society'. Society is regarded as being more important than individuals. This perspective has been popularised by Emile Durkheim.
Interactionism	Social behaviour is viewed as being generated by inventive and creative individuals. The actions of these individuals are considered to be more important than 'society'. This perspective has been popularised by Max Weber.
Conflict theory	This sociological perspective focuses upon economic relations within societies. These economic relations are considered to determine the nature of society. Karl Marx has made the perspective famous.

be traced back to these philosophers. There follows a summary of each of the above perspectives in order to develop the definitions within the previous table. Each of the key perspectives is defined, key figures influencing the perspective are identified and central terms within each perspective are explained.

Functionalism

Functionalists such as Emile Durkheim regard society (or societies) as being of more importance than individuals. The perspective gets its name from asking about how social institutions such as 'the family' and 'the political system' make society function. The perspective begins from the assumption that every society has a number of basic needs if it is to survive. An example of such a 'need' is the importance of social order. Functionalists consider that social order is not possible unless there are shared norms and values. These shared norms and values can only become widely accepted through socialising individuals. This means that functionalists are interested in identifying the ways that order is established within society.

This way of visualising society means that functionalists are interested in the social components that combine to give a society its definition. This means that social institutions such as the family, the health system, the education system and the political and religious institutions of society become critically important in establishing social order.

Functionalists are also interested in conflict and social disorder. The forces that are contrary to the established order are a part of many social systems. Functionalists are interested in the ways in which the social system deals with negative social factors to the extent that they become a manageable part of the social world. The presence of social disorder raises a criticism of functionalism. Taylor (2004, p15) criticises the perspective for 'presenting a deterministic picture of social behaviour'. This is because of the functionalist focus on social systems forming individuals. The reason why this functionalist approach is open to criticism rests in the social disorder that many individuals can experience. If the social system is to be omnipotent in the way that authors such as Orwell (1949) have popularised, there could never be the conscious rejection of so many social values that have been highlighted by the UK media in 2007. This suggests that if one focuses on the importance of the social system to the detriment of acknowledging the importance of creative individuals making choices, one is excluding a massively significant part of social interaction.

CASE STUDY

The Bowman family live in an inner city council estate. Within the estate there are problems with unemployment, crime, drug and alcohol addiction. The family include Angela Bowman who is a single mother with three children (Ann (eight) Michelle (seven) and Dean (four)). Ann, and Dean both receive support for their special educational needs. Dean has already been cautioned for aggressive behaviour at his local nursery and Ann has had a number of episodes of 'challenging behaviour' at her local school. Michelle is different from Ann and Dean. She seems to be a gentle and shy girl who is naturally good at reading, writing and numeracy. Michelle seems to be the complete opposite to Ann. Angela explains the difference between Michelle and the other children by reasoning that 'the beauty of children is that they're all different'.

REFLECTIVE TASK

How does the case study contradict functionalism?

FEEDBACK

We have said that functionalists are interested in looking at how social groups influence individuals. This means that this sociological theory emphasises the importance of the 'big picture' as opposed to looking at how individuals create and generate social meaning. The Bowman family do appear to have been influenced by social factors. It could be argued that the challenging behaviour of Ann and Dean is a product of the negative social environment that is being experienced by the family. The difficulty of this argument is that the same social factors appear to have influenced Michelle in a very different way. Michelle is described as being 'gentle and shy'. This appears to indicate that individuals are not entirely a product of social forces. It suggests that the individual characteristics of each person may be a product of forces that are unrelated to wider social environment.

Interactionism

Interactionists such as Max Weber focus on how individuals interact with each other. In some respects this means that this perspective is opposed to functionalism. Taylor (2004, p17) proposes that within interactionism an emphasis is placed on negotiating meanings. This means that human encounters are not considered to be 'fixed'. They are visualised as being dependent on the negotiation of those individuals involved in the encounter. Whereas functionalists such as Durkheim emphasise the importance of the social system, interactionists are concerned with the negotiated meanings that develop during the process of interaction. This process is visualised as being creative as individual human actors interpret the social system in an inventive way.

Interactionism is allied to Symbolic Interactionism. This sociological perspective emphasises the importance of how people use symbols within interaction. Speech is regarded as being a particularly important symbolic way of guiding, interpreting and making sense of interaction. Taylor (2004, p17) is critical of this sociological perspective because of the focus on 'small-scale interaction'. This means that the implications of wider social trends are not necessarily taken into consideration. It can also mean that interactionist studies become impressionistic and localised so that they are open to the accusation that they are unable to obtain global findings.

REFLECTIVE TASK

Think about your own personal development. To what extent do you think that your personality has been formed by the social system? To what extent do you think that your personality is a product of negotiated meanings with other social actors?

FEEDBACK

A way of resolving this 'either/or' dilemma is to view your personality as having been influenced by a combination factors. In other words the person is a product of both the wider social system and negotiated meanings with other social actors. This means that neither one perspective nor the other has the complete answer to the question of how our personality is formed. Both of the perspectives are correct to draw attention to the variables influencing personal development. Their effectiveness is heightened if they are used in tandem to account for individual development.

Conflict theory

Conflict theory has been influenced by the ideas of Karl Marx. It is a sociological perspective that is similar to functionalism because of the emphasis that is placed upon the social system. Conflict theory differs from functionalism because there is not a focus on social consensus. The perspective investigates the conflict existing within social systems as opposed to studying the factors producing social harmony. Taylor (2004, p15) emphasises the importance of the concept 'ideology' to conflict theory. Ideology is visualised as being the beliefs and values which disguise truth and distort the reality of the social system. This ideology is considered as supporting the values of the rich and powerful. It is regarded as being opposed to the social system's poor and powerless.

Karl Marx popularised the notion of looking at the contradictory elements of social systems. Marx also popularised the terms 'infrastructure' and 'superstructure'. Whereas the infrastructure refers to all tangible aspects of the economic system, the superstructure refers to systems of belief and ideas. According to Marx, this economic infrastructure is responsible for shaping the beliefs and ideas of the superstructure. Marx also popularised the idea of social classes. The traditional Marxist emphasis is on the existence of two main social groups, a ruling class and a subject class who are considered as being in conflict with each other. Marx argues that there are fundamental contradictions within modern industrial societies such as the UK. The exemplification of such contradictory relationships can be seen in the traditional working arrangements for factories. Whereas the workers are traditionally 'on the factory floor', the factory manager is usually based in a private office. Another example of a contradictory relationship occurs with private ownership. A few powerful individuals own companies whereas the majority of the population own very little in comparison to these powerful individuals. Marx argues that the many contradictions in society produce instability and conflict. This is the rationale behind the prediction that a revolution will occur within capitalist societies so that the social order can be refined into a communist society.

Marxism is a profound and complex social theory. The emphasis on 'conflict' is testimony to the influence of Hegel's philosophical idea of the social world being characterised by 'thesis, antithesis and synthesis'. It is acknowledged that a social revolution will only occur when the working class become fully aware of the unfair contradictions that exist within the social system. The argument runs that until this realisation occurs, the social system is likely to survive because of the 'false-consciousness' of the working class. It is only when the working class become fully aware of the implications of social contradictions and of the need to replace the existing social order with a communist society that a social revolution will occur.

REFLECTIVE TASK

Why do you think that Marx's prediction that there will be a revolution in capitalist societies has only happened in a few capitalist social systems?

> ### FEEDBACK
>
> *It can be argued that a difficulty with the traditional Marxist focus on the economic infrastructure is that it neglects the creativity of individuals. It is too prescriptive in that the assumption is made that social contradictions will lead to a revolution and a new social order. Individuals will not necessarily react in the way that Marx predicted when there is the potential for meanings to be negotiated. The false consciousness that Marx writes about may be perpetuated when individuals are content to maintain the existing social system. Marx thought that false consciousness would lead to a revolution once the proletariat became educated and politicised. In the UK there are many people who reject politics. They are not prepared to be part of what is deemed to be 'spin' and 'lies'. It is not necessarily accurate to refer to this state of mind as false consciousness. It appears to be the case that individuals have a large number of choices available to them. Revolution is one possible choice that seems to be rejected because it is associated with political movements that have lost their credibility. Although there may be a significant number of people who are not as content as they could be, they do not necessarily feel so discontented that a revolution is likely to result.*

Applying sociology to Early Years

The three sociological perspectives that have been introduced within this chapter can be applied to Early Years. They offer a number of insights into society and provide a further level of skills whereby professional practice can be informed by social theory. If this raised awareness of the importance of social factors is combined with the applied psychological theory discussed in Chapter 1, there is the possibility of an even more profound holistic therapy combining psychological and sociological ideas. This next section of the chapter introduces some of the ways that you can apply sociological ideas to the Early Years context.

Functionalism and Early Years

In the previous section of the chapter we defined functionalism as being a sociological perspective that is concerned with social systems in relation to how consensus is maintained. This macro approach focuses on the wider social picture by drawing attention to the impact of wider society on children and families. The emphasis is placed on how children and families are affected by social structures such as the education system, the health system and the political system. In the UK there was some limited social security before 1946. National Insurance had been introduced in 1911, old age pensions for people over 70 in 1908, and workers who paid National Insurance could receive free medical treatment if they registered with a doctors' panel. This pivotal date (1946) is the time when the welfare state became such an important part of UK social policy. William Beveridge's notion of a welfare state looking after the needs of children and families from birth until death became a dominant idea within UK society from 1942 onwards. This notion of the welfare state led to the introduction of the NHS, social security and social services. This meant that there was a formal recognition that the wider social system has a massive impact upon the lives of children and families.

It is important for Early Years practitioners to acknowledge that the social system has a massive impact on the life chances of children and families. It can be argued that the relatively affluent life style enjoyed by many UK people is a product of the welfare state. This means that it is important for Early Years practitioners to become as fully aware as possible of the state services that are available to help children and families. As opposed to accepting that responsibility rests with individuals to be 'self-reliant' it is important to acknowledge that life chances are heavily influenced by the type of society that has been created. This argument is justified by considering the many problems that are experienced by children and families living in countries that do not have a welfare state. If the social system is underdeveloped so that individual families become accountable for their life chances there are fewer opportunities for those children and families who are unable to look after their own interests.

This means that Early Years practitioners need to be aware of the importance of having robust social agencies that are able to plan for and coordinate effective health care and education. This does not mean that it is necessary for Early Years practitioners to become political activists! It is more of a need to learn the lessons of history. The welfare state has improved the life chances of many children and families so this means that it is important to acknowledge the importance of wider social structures being able to help those who cannot help themselves.

The following case study example outlines the ways in which the functionalist awareness of the social system can be applied to Early Years.

CASE STUDY

The Njemba family arrived in the UK after spending seven years in Nairobi. Mr and Mrs Njemba have three children aged seven, five and three. The family have become used to being reliant on each other because of the difficulties with the infrastructure in Nairobi. They used to live in a poor district of the city. There were no shops in this area, no running water and no school for the children until last year. A Roman Catholic missionary organisation established a school for the children and the benefits of a basic education persuaded the Njembas to move to the UK. Although the family have immigrated into the country illegally they are still sure that there are many benefits to living in the UK. They are able to enjoy a much more robust infrastructure. There is running water and employment opportunities. Although the Njembas are not considered to be official UK citizens they think that they have many more social benefits living illegally in London than they ever did as legal citizens in Nairobi. The family attend mass at a local Catholic Church and their children already receive a number of social and educational benefits from being part of this religious community. Each Sunday there is a 'children's liturgy' and the children get to use pens, paper, books and musical instruments. One of the parishioners is a foreman in a local factory and he has told Mr Njemba that there is the possibility of 'casual labour'. The Njembas think that their life opportunities are dramatically different within a social system that appears to offer so many opportunities.

REFLECTIVE TASK

How can functionalism be applied to this case study?

FEEDBACK

In the case-study about the Bowman family we said that functionalists are not able to explain every aspect of child development because there are 'non-social' factors that also influence children. The above case-study does, however, reveal the potential importance that a child's social environment can have on its development. When a social system has a poorly developed infrastructure, this is likely to have profound consequences for the child's development. Once the Njemba family move to a society with an improved infrastructure, there are more opportunities for the family and these opportunities (both economic and social) help the children's physical, intellectual, emotional and social development.

Interactionism and Early Years

In contrast to functionalism, the interactionist perspective emphasises the importance of individuals. There is less focus on macro sociological structures and much more attention paid to the ways in which individuals negotiate meaning during their social encounters. This sociological perspective is important for Early Years because it reinforces the importance of meeting the individual needs of children. The interactionist approach to sociology would endorse any practice that aims to treat children as individuals, with the potential to grow and develop as long as this opportunity is presented to them. Even the word 'sociology' appears to emphasise the importance of studying groups of individuals as opposed to focusing on the meanings that are negotiated by social actors. To apply an analogy, it is as if the 'individual trees' are being missed because of the focus on the 'wider wood'. It can be argued that effective Early Years practice cannot be characterised by looking at major social structures because the individual needs of children and families are likely to be missed if this is the prevalent approach to practice. The interactionist approach to sociology begins by asking how individuals interpret the social world and in turn negotiate social meanings. If Early Years practitioners adopt a similar philosophy, individual children and their rights are likely to become central to practice. This theme is emphasised in Nigel Parton's (2005) text. It is considered to be vital that children's individual needs are central to practice if quality child care provision is to be given.

If an interactionist approach to Early Years work is adopted it is also more likely that the creativity of children will be acknowledged and incorporated into effective practice. It can be argued that an interactionist perspective may be more prepared to value the importance 'free-play' because of the emphasis that is put on each child nurturing their individual creativity. Play techniques that stimulate the child's imagination are also likely to be considered to be important to children's growth and development if one adopts an interactionist perspective. This is because of the emphasis that is placed on meanings being negotiated by creative individuals. Some of the benefits of an interactionist approach to Early Years practice are outlined in the following case study.

CASE STUDY

Amanda has recently completed a PGCE and she is in her first teaching post in a primary school. Amanda has studied a number of educational theories and she is particularly interested in the ideas of the psychologist Howard Gardner and his concept of 'multiple intelligences'. Amanda has adapted Gardner's work to devise a questionnaire that assesses individual children's learning preferences. Amanda has used this questionnaire with children aged six to seven. She has created a learning profile for the class and this is used in order to organise teaching sessions. Amanda sets tasks for the children according to their learning preference. She has found that the children have made much progress since she has been responding to their individual learning needs. As well as feeling valued, the children are able to complete tasks that appear to be appropriate to their individual needs. This positive teaching experience has made Amanda even more concerned about the National Curriculum. She considers it to be a global approach to education when it would seem to be much more important to meet individual needs.

REFLECTIVE TASK

How can interactionism be applied to this case study?

FEEDBACK

We have emphasised that interactionists emphasise the importance of individuals and their ability to create and negotiate social meanings. The 'personalised learning activities' that are being applied within the case study appear to support what interactionism says. As opposed to emphasising the importance of the social group, interactionism places an emphasis on the importance of the individual. In this case study, each learner has an individualised learning profile and this becomes the means of developing learning. It can be argued that supporters of interactionism are likely to have reservations about a 'national curriculum' that places the goals of the social group before the needs of individuals.

Conflict theory and Early Years

We said in the previous section of the chapter that conflict theorists are interested in how social systems deal with social conflict. We also noted that the most famous strand of conflict theory applies the ideas of Karl Marx in explaining the social environment. This means that conflict theory has become associated with economics, in particular the ways that economic conflicts within social systems influence social interaction. This aspect of conflict theory is relevant to Early Years because of the relationship that exists between a child's economic circumstances and their ability to grow and develop. Although a number of factors influence child development it can be argued that economic circumstances are especially influential. We need only look at our society and the link that exists between economic wealth and children's educational achievement. Anthea Lipsett (2007) draws attention to the importance that the government has given to ensuring that the budgets that are given to schools enable them to resource 'world-class' learning and teaching. Early Years practitioners need to be aware that children can only fulfil their potential if their economic circumstances support their growth and development. This means that it is important to be aware of the economic circumstances of the children we are working with. Although the UK is a relatively wealthy country there are still children who do not have a satisfactory diet. A House of Commons Work and Pensions Committee report in 2003–2004 identified that 13 per cent of UK children experienced short-term poverty (1–3 years in poverty). These factors will have a massive impact upon how children grow and develop. If we adopt the philosophy of conflict theorists we can argue that if these economic circumstances are alleviated there are more opportunities for the children to reach their developmental potential.

CASE STUDY

James is six and comes from an inner city housing complex. His mother is unemployed and their only form of income is 'social security'. Although James is an only child, his mother finds it very difficult to manage financially. Christmas is an especially difficult time because James is very aware of other children getting expensive presents. James is a malnourished child who often only has cereal before school. This means that he finds it difficult to concentrate in school. He does have a hot meal when he gets in from school but the quality of this food is not as good as it could be. James also feels the cold because his mother has been unable to get a warm winter coat for him. These material circumstances mean that James is unable to reach his educational potential. He likes books and reading but his access to books is limited compared to some of the other children in his class. James is also starting to show some signs of low self-esteem. He notices what the other children have and listens to them talking about what they do when they are not in school. This has made James feel that he is different. His best friend Will is going to 'Euro Disney' in the spring but James has never been on a family holiday. His mother does take him to the local park in the summer holidays but James wishes he could do something else. The world that he sees on television appears to be very different from the reality of the life he leads with his unemployed mother.

REFLECTIVE TASK

How can conflict theory be applied to this case study?

FEEDBACK

It could be argued that many of the difficulties that James is experiencing would be resolved if his material circumstances were improved. James is described as being 'malnourished' and this poor diet will influence his development. Although James may be a 'bright' child, his material circumstances may also be the main reason why he has feelings of 'low self-esteem'. Although 'materialism' may bring as many social problems as poverty, it would still appear to be the case that child development is profoundly influenced by the distribution of a country's wealth. In a situation of 'haves' and 'have nots' a redistribution of wealth can mean that child development improves and a more equalitarian society is thus produced.

REFLECTIVE TASK

Think about each of the sociological perspectives outlined in Table 2.1 and suggest what would interest them about 'child poverty'.

FEEDBACK

Each of the sociological perspectives would explain child poverty differently. Functionalist sociologists would be interested in the threats that are posed to the social system by poverty. Threats to the social system are regarded as being 'dysfunctional'. This means that it is important for the social system to be able to activate a strategy in order to counter the negative impact of child poverty. The social system is regarded as being similar to a biological organism. It is proposed that in a way that is similar to the activation of the immune system there are ways of restoring the social equilibrium. Functionalists would be interested in the ways that the social system's economy responds to child poverty. The argument would run that because child poverty produces instability, the social system will need to redirect economic resources to counter this problem. If there is no end to child poverty there is no way that the social system will be able to operate effectively. This may lead to the ultimate collapse of the social system and the establishment of a new social order.

Interactionist sociologists are interested in how social actors negotiate meanings. This understanding of sociology means that it is assumed that the consequences of child poverty will differ from one individual to the next. The perspective is interested in how individuals form creative strategies in order to negotiate social challenges. This means that interactionist sociologists would account for child poverty by saying that the problem is more or less pronounced according to the strategies that are employed by individuals. Just as there are some innovative individuals who are able to escape from the effects of child poverty, so there are also individuals who are unable to counter its effects.

Conflict theorists would be interested in the social disorder that is generated by child poverty. Marxist sociologists explain child poverty as being an inevitable consequence of the capitalist economic system. This economic system places 'capital' (land, industry and money) in the hands of a few dominant individuals. This means that child poverty is experienced by the majority of the population. Conflict theorists would also argue that child poverty will be one of the reasons why the capitalist economic system will be overthrown once its extent is fully known.

PRACTICAL TASK

When you are next on the Internet do a word search for 'functionalism', 'interactionism' and 'conflict theory'. Try to find out more information about the main individuals who are associated with the perspectives (Emile Durkheim, Max Weber and Karl Marx). Make a note of what would interest the three sociologists about your own Early Years setting.

We can now complete our introductory chapter by focusing our discussion on critically appraising the sociological perspectives in terms of their value for Early Years.

Critical appraisal of how sociological theory can be used in Early Years settings

As with psychology, there is no one perspective that provides all the possible answers to the questions that we may have about the social development of children. The most effective way of applying sociological perspectives to Early Years appears to be combining their relative merits in order to present a holistic approach to understanding child development.

Appraising functionalism

All three perspectives highlighted in this chapter have strengths and weaknesses. The functionalist approach with its focus on 'social systems' can make the mistake of emphasising the importance of the social system so that the actions of individuals are not fully taken into consideration. The danger of this approach can mean that the social system is depicted in such a way that it appears to be removed from the actions of individuals. This means that although it is correct to draw attention to the 'wider picture' it is also important to acknowledge how individuals manipulate the social system in a creative way in order to produce 'negotiated meanings'. Lopez and Scott (2000, p17) draw attention to the importance of acknowledging individual actions in 'modern societies'. This is because this social context is characterised by individuals being 'far more differentiated from one another'. Lopez and Scott (2000, p17) go on to say that 'social action in these circumstances is characterised by a high level of institutionalised individualism'. This means that the general functionalist focus on a macro social order is limited because it can only explain the actions of social systems as opposed to fully accounting for the actions of creative individuals.

Appraising interactionism

It can also be argued that are also limitations with the interactionist focus upon 'negotiated meanings'. It is important to acknowledge the impact that individuals have in generating social meaning in order to address the functionalist over-emphasis on 'social systems'. It may be suggested, however, that interactionists can be inclined to exaggerate the importance of individual interpretations of the social order. Lopez and Scott (2000, p29) make the important point that although 'individual minds' are important in holding 'knowledge', this knowledge is not isolated but 'shared by those who interact together'. A similar point is made by Davis:

> An individual carries his social position in his head, so to speak, and puts it into action when the appropriate occasion arises. Not only does he carry it in his head but others also carry it in theirs, because social positions are matters of reciprocal expectation and must be publicly and commonly perceived by everyone in the group. (1948, p87)

This means that it is important to acknowledge the role that others play in generating social meaning. It can be argued that this focus is potentially lost by the interactionist concern with 'the individual' who may be seen in isolation from 'the social group'. A further criticism of interactionism concerns the implication that individuals are 'all important'. This is similar to Margaret Thatcher's phrase that 'there is no such thing as society, there are individual men, women and families'. This emphasis on the individual can come at the expense of neglecting the importance of the social system. It is an idea that goes against many aspects of good practice within Early Years because it is denying the important role that the social system has in helping to nurture and develop children.

Appraising conflict theory

It is also possible to criticise conflict theory in a similar way to the other two perspectives. This is because this sociological perspective, like functionalism and interactionism can be accused as having a one dimensional approach to explaining social systems. This is especially true with Marxist perspectives that often reduce their explanation for social phenomena to economic variables. Lopez and Scott (2000, p80) argue that the work of Habermas offers a potential solution to the tendency to focus on either 'the social system' or 'the actions of individuals' or 'the economy'. Habermas (1981) suggests that the social structure is influenced by both 'communicative action' and 'purposive action'. According to Habermas, communicative action corresponds to attaining mutual understanding between the participants of a social system. In contrast, purposive action is directed towards achieving goals by more independent and 'strategic and calculative ways'. This means that as well as the shared social meanings of social systems there are also the creative interpretations of individuals who may manipulate the social system in order to realise particular goals. It can be argued that this synthesis of functionalist, interactionist and conflict theorist thought provides a potential means of resolving the 'either or' debate.

CHAPTER SUMMARY

In this chapter we have seen that sociology is not 'common sense explained in an oblique way'. It is a discipline that has a rich philosophical heritage with competing interpretations of the social world. Like psychology, there are a number of sociological perspectives and each one has its own interpretation of the social world. The chapter has defined and explored three especially influential perspectives that are of use to Early Years practice. The particular relevance of these perspectives for the Early Years context has been explored and a critical appraisal of each of the perspectives has been given. As with psychology it can be argued that the best way to apply sociology to Early Years is to combine the perspectives so that the complex needs of individuals are more likely to be met. If this is done, it is possible to have the holistic approach to meeting individual needs that has been identified in the previous chapter. This would appear to be the best way of applying sociology to Early Years.

Self-assessment questions

1   Name three influential sociological perspectives?

2   How can Early Years workers apply sociological perspectives to help children and maximise their professional practice?

3   Give an example strength and weakness of each of the sociological perspectives that have been referred to in this chapter.

Moving on

This chapter has introduced you to the idea of 'perspectives' or 'paradigms' of sociological thought. Try to become familiar with this term. The research process chapter also deals with the idea that there are competing models of thought that shape the nature of the individual social science disciplines. This is a key term that will enrich your knowledge of social science in general.

REFERENCES

Audi, R. (1995) *The Cambridge dictionary of philosophy*. Cambridge: Cambridge University Press.

Berger, P. (1966) *Invitation to sociology*. London: Hamondsworth.

Davis, K. (1948) *Human society*. New York: Macmillan.

Durkheim, E. (1952) *Suicide: a study in sociology*. London: Routledge & Kegan Paul.

Gardner, H. (1985) *Frames of mind: the theory of multiple intelligence*. New York: Basic Books.

Habermas, J. (1981) *The theory of communicative action*. London: Heinemann.

House of Commons Work and Pensions Committee (Online: www. publications.parliament.uk).

Lipsett, A (2007) Darling announces extra education spend. (Online: www. education.guardian.co.uk).

Lopez, J. and Scott, J. (2000) *Social structure*. Buckingham. Open University Press.

Marshall, G. (1994) *Oxford dictionary of sociology*. Oxford: Oxford University Press.

Mills, C.W. (1959) *The sociological imagination*. Oxford. Oxford University Press.

Online dictionary. (Online: www.dictionary.reference.com).

Orwell, G. (1949) *Nineteen eighty-four*. London: Penguin Books Ltd.

Parton, N. (2005) *Safeguarding children: early intervention and surveillance in late modern society*. London: Palgrave Macmillan.

Taylor, P., Richardson, J., Yeo, A., Marsh, I., Trobe, K., and Pilkington, A. (2004) Sociology in *focus*. Ormskirk. Causeway Press.

Telegraph Online, 15 October 2007. (Online: www.telegraph.co.uk).

FURTHER READING

Taylor, P., Richardson, J., Yeo, A., Marsh, I., Trobe, K., and Pilkington, A (2004) *Sociology in focus*. London: Causeway Press.
An excellent textbook in terms of clarity of content and analysis but the material is not always related to Early Years contexts.

Yeo, A. and Lovell, T. (2003) *Sociology for childhood studies*. London: Hodder & Stoughton.
An excellent textbook that is written in an accessible way and makes clear links to applying sociology to Early Years contexts.

3 Social policy and Early Years

CHAPTER OBJECTIVES

After reading this chapter you should be able to:
- analyse how social policy impacts upon the professional practice of Early Years practitioners.

The chapter develops your knowledge and understanding of social policy and how it can be applied to the Early Years context. The chapter content is relevant to the standards that are referred to in Chapter 2 ('S2', 'S3', 'S8', 'S29' and 'S38') because these standards require you to reflect on the social factors influencing child development. The chapter explains what social policy is and then explores how selected social policies can be applied to the Early Years context. There are a number of factors that have influenced the creation of social policies so some of these factors are considered within the chapter. The chapter follows a similar structure to the first two chapters as there are formative activities that develop your learning in relation to the main chapter themes.

Introduction

Social policies are made by the state in order to regulate the social world. These policies have been influenced by politicians and other influential social thinkers over time. It can be argued that social policy is a particularly important area of interest for Early Years practitioners because of the extent of the influence that social policies have on the interaction that occurs between professionals, children and families. This chapter explores these themes. Before we look at the development of UK social policy and explore the impact that these social policies have had on the professional interaction of Early Years practitioners, it is important to consider what the term 'social policy' means.

What is social policy?

Social policy is defined by Alcock (2000, p1) as being 'the practical application and implementation of those policies we consider to be social'. It can be argued that this is a workable definition of social policy because social policy has direct consequences for children and families. This means that social policy is concerned with the welfare or well-being of individuals. Alcock (2000, p2) develops this definition by arguing that UK social policy is especially concerned with five aspects of welfare. Alcock names these five areas of concern as 'income maintenance and social security, health policy and services, the personal social services, education and training policy, and employment policy and housing policy'. In terms of the academic content of social policy, Alcock (2000, p2) argues that it is a subject that is informed by 'sociology, economics, politics, policy making and history'.

REFLECTIVE TASK

Which aspects of social policy do you consider to be especially relevant to Early Years?

FEEDBACK

The previous explanation of the characteristics of social policy identifies five areas of particular importance. All five of these areas have implications for children and families. This means that they (income maintenance and social security, health policy and services, the personal social services, education and training policy, and employment policy and housing) are all particularly important for Early Years. One of the most important needs of any child is to develop. All five of the areas of social policy that Alcock (2000, p2) identifies are especially important for child development. It is particularly important that children live in households that have enough money to provide for their needs. It is also important to provide children with effective health, and social care, so that their educational needs are met in order to enable their future employment and social needs.

The social policy process

If social policies are to be introduced in order to solve social problems, and if they are to be evaluated as being 'effective' one can apply a cyclical process of analysis. This is referred to by Alcock (2000, p3) as 'the policy cycle'. The process involves identifying a social need, proposing policy solutions, implementing these policy solutions and ultimately evaluating their effectiveness.

This means that social policy is not just a study of society and its problems. It is an area of study that it is intimately concerned with how to act upon and improve social problems. The social institutions that are created to ensure that social problems are resolved are also of central importance to social policy. It can be argued that a central part of the social policy process is to look at the role of the state in relation to its effectiveness in providing for its citizens.

REFLECTIVE TASK

How can the 'policy cycle' of 'identifying needs, proposing solutions, implementing solutions and evaluating solutions' be put into effect within Early Years?

Chapter 6 explains the research process within social science. One of the main ways of identifying social problems is to complete research into social life in order to identify those aspects of society that are working and those areas that are responsible for generating social problems. If 'needs' are to be identified it is important to ensure that accurate research about social issues is completed. This research can be used to form the basis of the evidence that can be presented to identify the important social problems that need to be resolved. Anne Watson (2004) discusses the challenges that exist within the UK educational curriculum. It would appear that part of the challenge of education within the UK is to produce a situation where teachers and learners have shared views on what is important and unimportant. We could propose that if a new educational curriculum was introduced into the UK that promoted social responsibility, this might help to change some of the lack of achievement that is being experienced within UK educational institutions. If this policy direction was adopted by UK educational policy makers it could be monitored and in turn evaluated in the hope of producing solutions to educational challenges.

The concept of partnership

Anthony Giddens (2004) argues that the concept of 'partnership' characterises New Labour's approach to social policy. This means that all the sectors of the 'mixed economy of care' (statutory, private, voluntary and informal) are being encouraged to work together.

REFLECTIVE TASK

Write out a definition for the statutory, private, voluntary and informal sectors of care provision.

FEEDBACK

The following table defines the four sectors of care.

Table 3.1 Defining the mixed economy of care

Sector of care	Definition	Examples
Statutory	The statutory sector includes all of the services that are financed and organised by the government.	Examples of statutory services include schools, the NHS, and state social services.
Private	The private sector includes all of the services that operate to make a financial profit.	Examples of private services include private nurseries and private schools.

Table 3.1 Continued

Sector of care	Definition	Examples
Voluntary	The voluntary sector operates according to 'good will'.	Voluntary organisations include charities such as 'Barnados' and 'Childline'.
Informal	The informal sector is characterised by family and friends caring for each other because of 'love' and/or 'obligation'.	Parents caring for children and friends caring for each other are examples of 'informal' care.

New Labour's ideal model of partnership is revealed in Figure 3.1.

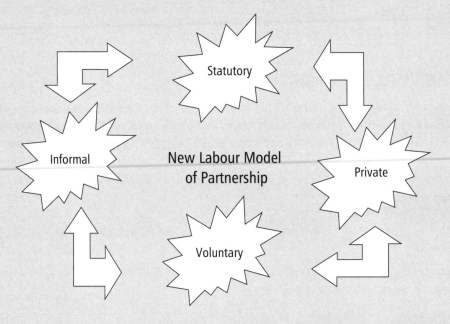

This model of care has evolved due to a number of social, political, historical and economic factors. The heritage of the mixed economy of care is discussed in the next section of the chapter.

Historical factors influencing social policy

A number of factors have influenced UK social policy from 1834 onwards. All social policies have been influenced by historical factors. In this country, ideas about society have evolved over time. This means that philosophical, economic, and sociological interpretations of society have developed and informed social policy. Harris (2004, p1) phrases this as being the 'ideological life' that informs the social world. It can be argued that this 'ideological life' is at the centre of many of the UK's social policies.

The 1834 Poor Law Amendment Act and the workhouse

Prior to 1834, the 'Speenhamland System' had been in place. The parish of Speenhamland near to Newbury in Berkshire developed the practice of giving poor relief in cash to supplement inadequate wages. After 1834, the 'workhouse' replaced this policy. This new approach to social policy was introduced by Edwin Chadwick who criticised the Speenhamland system for being 'too generous' to the poor.

The Poor Law Amendment Act of 1834 represents an important development in social welfare. This policy introduced a system of 'workhouses' to address the social problem of 'poverty'. The workhouse system meant that in order to receive financial help from the state an individual had to work in an institution called a workhouse. Harris (2004, p52) considers the legislation to be a 'watershed in British social policy history'. This is because this social policy conflicts with previous 'laissez-faire' approaches to welfare. 'Laissez-faire' refers to the unwillingness of the state to intervene in social life. This French phrase refers to the philosophy of 'non-intervention' where individuals are 'left to do' what have they have to, in order to 'make ends meet'. This philosophy characterised the state's response to social policy within the UK prior to 1834.

Following the 1834 Poor Law, a distinction was made between the 'deserving' and the 'undeserving' poor. The legislation developed the 1601 'poor laws' that were designed to punish the 'undeserving' poor. As a result of the legislation, anyone receiving financial help from the state became a virtual social outcast. They became stigmatised, or labelled 'social lepers'. This meant that the 1834 Poor Law increased the feelings of shame the individual experienced if they claimed benefits from the state. To be eligible for state help, the individual had to give up their 'personal liberty' or 'citizen's rights'.

The 1834 Poor Law is significant because it introduced an important idea in social policy, the notion of a 'means test'. The 'means test' assesses the eligibility of the claimant to receive benefits. From 1834 onwards, UK social policy makers have considered 'personal circumstances' in relation to entitlement to benefits. This notion has been encouraged by a number of influential governments. The workhouse system was based on this belief. To receive any state help a person had to live and work in a workhouse.

REFLECTIVE TASK

What do you think it would have been like to have been in a 'workhouse'?

It is possible to imagine what it would have been like living in a workhouse if you think of the images of Victorian society that were created by Charles Dickens. The famous novel Oliver Twist portrays a world of fear, hunger, illness, and poverty. The workhouse may be associated with all of these terms. As opposed to a 'caring system' that puts into effect the Rogerian principles that have been discussed in Chapter 1, the workhouse appears to be opposed to 'client-centred therapy'. The Dickensian images of society never appear to have 'disease, ignorance, idleness, squalor and want' too far removed from social life. This gives the impression that the workhouse system was wholly ineffective in meeting the needs of the poor.

The influence of Victorian morality on social policy

Queen Victoria lived from 1819–1901 and was monarch at a time when Britain's foreign policy was dominated by imperialism. It can be argued that the influence of the Victorian era on social policy is important. Religion was a particularly important component of Victorian life. This led to the influence of the concept of 'Victorian morality' on social policy. It can be argued that the popular perception was that it was important to 'work hard for a living and obey the ten commandments of the Bible'. The poor were treated with 'charity' or 'kindness'. They were given help but never too much help. This meant that a 'carrot and stick' approach characterised social policy. A little was given but never too much in case the poor became dependent upon charity. This leads Harris to argue that although 'philanthropy' or charity is an important aspect of nineteenth- century social policy, 'it would be wrong to ignore its limitations' (2004, p72).

The importance of the institution

The Victorians designed enormous institutions to house those needing care. This meant that 'patients' became separated from the rest of society. The 'insane' were regarded as being 'morally wrong'. A family that had a child with disabilities was seen as being punished by God for some 'wrong' they had committed. It can be argued that Victorian society was a 'controlling society'. Scull (1982, p198) reveals that the number of patients who were admitted to 'types of asylum' rose from 7,000 in 1855 to over 16,000 by 1890. This 'controlling system' is also revealed by the example of the Jeremy Bentham 'panopticon', an instrument of surveillance that was designed so that staff could see into every cell with a system of mirrors and observe every action of the person in 'care'.

As a result of this approach to social policy, many people avoided getting help from the state. A further problem was that although the Victorians built large institutions in order to 'incarcerate' those requiring care, large numbers of people still needed help from the informal sector of relatives and friends. As well as the expense of placing patients in institutions, the 'care' that was given to these patients was based on punitive principles. Harris (2004, p101) argues that medical procedures were based on 'restraints and fear'. These procedures began to be applied to increasing numbers of people. By the end of the

Victorian era, 8 per cent of the population aged over 65 were institutionalised in work-houses, homes for older people, or hospitals and infirmaries. This compares to fewer than 3 per cent today (Blakemore, 2003).

Why do you think the 'asylum model' has been discontinued?

As well as the expense of building and maintaining large institutions, it can be argued that the 'asylum' is not the best way of caring for the mentally ill. Ken Kesey (1962) and Sylvia Plath (1963) have written about the 'harsh' regimes of 'care' that have been found in the asylums. These institutions were often located away from towns and cities as the 'mentally ill' became literally separated from society. The moral objection to this approach is that if we segregate those who have mental health needs we are 'dehumanising' the mentally ill because we are not including them in social interaction.

Social policy in the twentieth century: the Liberal government 1906–1914

The Speenhamland system and the 1834 Poor Law Amendment Act both represent important points in the development of social policy legislation. This is because many current social policies (for example 'Disability Living Allowance') have been influenced by this earlier legislation's theme of 'personal responsibility'. Both examples of legislation reveal a move away from 'laissez-faire' as the state began to acquire more responsibility for the welfare of its citizens. Nevertheless, the theme of 'individual responsibility' has never been replaced by a notion that the state should become responsible for its citizens.

This view began to change from the beginning of the twentieth century through Britain's involvement in the Boer War (1899–1902) and the First World War (1914–1918). One third of these army recruits failed their medicals and the state of the nation's health led to increased calls for 'state intervention' in social life. The importance of 'national efficiency' became a prevalent policy theme of David Lloyd George's Liberal government. This concern with 'national efficiency' was considered alongside concern over the social unrest that was developing throughout Europe. Working class people were starting to riot over the appalling living conditions in a number of European towns and cities. This led Dicey (1962, p53) to argue that 'nineteenth century Britain experienced a transition from Benthamite individualism to collectivism'. This signalled the beginning of the end of 'laissez-faire'.

In Germany, Bismarck attempted to prevent social disorder by introducing social policies that would help working-class people. At the beginning of the twentieth century, David

Lloyd George visited Germany and took note of the German social benefits system because of the political credit that was gained by Bismarck. Lloyd George began to introduce similar reforms to Britain so that by 1911 there was the introduction of the first social insurance scheme in the form of a 'National Insurance Act'. The first part of the legislation dealt with insurance against loss of earnings through sickness and the second part dealt with unemployment insurance. These reforms may have been unpopular among employers who resented having to pay towards employees' insurance cover but they were popular among the electorate in general. Harris (2004, p165) comments that it was these reforms that 'played a major role in laying the foundations for the development of the welfare state in the twentieth century'.

REFLECTIVE TASK

If you had lived at the time of David Lloyd George, do you think you would have been pleased that the 'Liberal Reforms' had been introduced?

FEEDBACK

Your answer to the question would depend on who you are thinking of! If you were living in a poor urban district in poverty you would probably be pleased about the introduction of the Liberal reforms. Harris (2004, p165) lists the main reforms as being 'the introduction of free school meals, the establishment of old age pensions and the creation of unemployment and health insurance schemes'. These reforms would have offered help and support for poor people. If you had benefited from 'laissez-faire' you might not have been so pleased about the Liberal reforms. The wealthy classes might have been threatened by the prospect of 'state welfare' because of the prospect of rising taxation. Like most social policies there are 'winners' and 'losers' according to whose view you are supporting!

The legacy of David Lloyd George

From 1900 to 1945 British society changed in many important ways. As well as David Lloyd George's social welfare reforms, women were allowed to vote. The country also witnessed the First World War from 1914–1918. This war was very different from other wars. The country's citizens suffered on a massive scale and the days of 'laissez-faire' (or lack of state intervention) could never to be repeated. Previous wars had not witnessed such a huge loss of life. Winter (1982, p72–73) reveals that by the end of 1918, 1.7 million British soldiers had been wounded and 723,000 had either died or been killed. This meant that the social welfare reforms of David Lloyd George gathered even more momentum. The population looked to the state to support them following a conflict that had affected most families.

The development of left-wing socialism

From 1800–1900 there was a change in demography in Britain. The working classes became established in the towns and cities. Prior to this time the country was predominantly 'agrarian' as opposed to being 'industrial'. After 1800, more people moved into the major towns and cities. Law (1967) reveals that between 1801 and 1851, the number of people living in towns of more than 10,000 inhabitants increased by more than 270 per cent. These people looked for work in industry and the political movement 'socialism' developed to help support the rights of working class people.

By 1918 we see a union between the concern for the need to have a compassionate, humane society seeking peaceful resolutions to conflict and a concern for the rights of working-class people. This led to socialism becoming increasingly important in the extent of its influence on social policy.

REFLECTIVE TASK

What do you think the political term 'socialism' means?

FEEDBACK

One way of remembering the meaning of 'socialism' is to recall the fable about 'Robin Hood' who 'took from the rich to give to the poor'! Socialism is a political idea that advocates 'taking from the rich' through taxation and 'giving to the poor' through establishing 'welfare services' such as state health, education, housing and social security. Whereas 'communism' advocates redistributing wealth from rich to poor through a revolution, socialism supports the same idea but recommends democratic ways as opposed to revolutionary action.

William Beveridge

Beveridge was a social reformer who urged Britain to create a new society in which everyone's needs would be met by the state. The tragedy of the First World War was exacerbated by the Second World War. Beveridge wanted to make Britain a 'New Jerusalem' or 'ideal state'. He aimed to do this by getting rid of what he described as key 'social evils' (disease, idleness, ignorance, squalor and want). The politicians who supported William Beveridge such as Clement Attlee believed that the way to do this was by having interventionist state policies. Harris (2004, p290) phrases this socialist strategy as 'an essentially gradualist approach to social change'.

This meant that implementing Beveridge's social policy recommendations became the opposite of 'laissez-faire' because they required huge amounts of spending on public services. The Labour Party of the 1940s embarked upon a campaign of public spending to get rid of Beveridge's 'social evils'. This led to the introduction of the NHS and council housing. It led to the expansion of state secondary education, social security and the introduction of statutory social services.

Beveridge's ideas were put into practice by a socialist Labour government in an attempt to change the nature of British society. Attlee's welfare state was based on the principle of ensuring equality of access to employment, education, and social services. These interventionist policies gained momentum from 1945–1979. This led to the statutory sector becoming the most important provider of welfare services. This development was also influenced by John Maynard Keynes (1883–1946). From 1946 the country's politicians attempted to implement Keynesian economics. Harris (2004, p292) summarises this approach to policy as 'acknowledgement of the idea that it was a legitimate part of the business of government to seek to ensure a high and stable level of employment'. Keynes argued that investing in public services would lead to the creation of employment because of the need to construct and staff hospitals, council houses, schools and colleges.

The indirect problems of Beveridge's Britain

It can be argued that Beveridge's interventionist welfare policy fuelled economic inflation. As more money was borrowed by the government to finance the welfare state, so wages and prices rose as this additional money became utilised. The unforeseen consequences of these social policies contributed to the economic inflation experienced by the UK economy in the second half of the twentieth century. This has meant that Beveridge has been criticised for being an 'idealist' with impractical ideas of achieving 'a new Jerusalem'.

REFLECTIVE TASK

Do you agree with the idea that Beveridge was 'an impractical idealist'?

FEEDBACK

You might agree with the suggestion that Beveridge was an 'idealist'. He recommended that the state should remove the 'five social evils' of disease, idleness, squalor, ignorance and want'. A society without these social evils would be 'ideal'! It can be argued that the practicalities of this approach to social welfare can be challenged. A society without disease, ignorance, squalor, idleness and want may be considered to be a 'utopia' of 'heaven on earth'. A realist might argue that this will never be possible because human societies can never be 'perfect places'.

Social policy, 1979–2001

Harris (2004, p303) argues that Mrs Thatcher's Conservatives made a number of significant changes to social policy from 1979. It could be argued that from 1979 onwards social policy moved away from state intervention and back to 'laissez-faire'. This was a signal that the days of highly interventionist government policies were coming to an end. Just as a number of complex factors led to the growth of the statutory sector, so there occurred a series of events that led to the dominance of a new philosophy of New Right Conservatism.

The importance of Milton Friedman

Milton Friedman is the American economist associated with 'monetarism'. Friedman's economic ideas are based on the principle that it is important to regulate the money that is spent on public services in order to achieve social stability. This means that Friedman's ideas are opposed to high levels of 'state public spending'. Mrs Thatcher was influenced by this idea and her government attempted to control or regulate the amount of money spent on 'public services'. Much of Mrs Thatcher's social policy legislation was based on monetarist principles. The rationale behind this approach was that controlling public spending would reduce inflation and that this in turn would reduce unemployment.

REFLECTIVE TASK

What do you think are the strengths and weaknesses of Friedman's monetarist ideas?

FEEDBACK

Friedman's recommendation to control levels of public expenditure may be seen as a 'strength' if it leads to lower levels of taxation. If the population have 'more money in their pockets' they might spend this money on goods and services. This is likely to stimulate economic growth. Reducing the government's public spending can also be regarded as a potential 'strength' because it will lower the amount of money that the government has to borrow to pay for welfare services. This is also potentially beneficial for the economy. The 'weakness' of this economic strategy is that the public sector will be given fewer resources. This may mean that the standard of welfare services is reduced. This was a major criticism of Mrs Thatcher's welfare legacy.

The NHS and Community Care Act of 1990

Mrs Thatcher's Conservatives became known as 'the New Right'. They attempted to run health, education and social care services as if they were 'businesses' in order to improve efficiency and to promote independence. This legislation led to a number of important consequences for public service. The next section of the chapter outlines some of the New Right's social policy reforms.

GP Fundholders

GP Fundholders were introduced under the New Right. This led to GPs being encouraged to apply for 'fundholding' status from the government. This meant that a GP became responsible for managing his/her own budget. The Conservatives thought that this was a good idea because it would lead to a GP having 'ownership' of the practice. This policy approach mirrored the private sector of 'managing directors' owning limited companies. The businessmen who advised Mrs Thatcher such as Lord Dearing and Lord Griffiths were influenced by the ergonomics of the American car manufacturer 'Ford'. Within 'Ford Motors' productivity was particularly high and part of the explanation that was given for this commercial success was that each worker was given much responsibility. It was argued that if GPs were given 'ownership of the process' through having financial responsibility, the quality of provision would improve. Opponents of the system argued that a two-tier system resulted, with GP Fundholders on one tier or level and everyone else on the next.

Trust status

The 1990 legislation led to the emergence of 'NHS Trusts'. Trusts acquired financial responsibilities. They received money from the government and they then had the expectation of managing this money. As opposed to being dependent upon the health authority, 'Trusts' such as hospitals and ambulance services became responsible for their own financial performance.

Purchasers, providers, commissioners

The emphasis placed upon financial responsibility led to a purchaser/provider model resulting. 'Purchasers' of health and care services such as GPs and social services bought care for their clients from health and social care providers such as hospitals and residential homes. The 'internal market' came into being as health, care and education became regulated by financial contracts.

New Labour: 1997

The criticisms of the purchaser/provider/commissioner model were one of the reasons why Tony Blair's 'New Labour' government swept to power in May 1997. Many UK citizens had become disillusioned with the New Right. New Labour promised that they would provide an alternative government, a 'third way' that would be a new combination of 'social compassion' and 'financial prudence'. A number of significant policy changes occurred in their first years of government.

The end of fundholding

All fundholding ended in December 1999. The new philosophical approach of 'partnership' replaced the view that health, care and education should be run like a business enterprise. This led to a move towards 'consensus management' or management through 'cooperation'.

The introduction of PCGs

This approach to health, care and education can be seen with the introduction of 'Primary Care Groups'. Shortly after New Labour's 1997 election victory, 'PCGs' became established. They comprised groups of local GPs serving a population of 100,000 patients. Their members came from GPs, representatives of social services and the voluntary sector. Their role was to meet together in order to coordinate and plan services together. Community nurses were given the role of 'commissioning' (or assessing local needs for services). This emphasis of cooperation as opposed to competition has become the dominant approach to social policy since 1997.

REFLECTIVE TASK

Write an essay of between 800–1,000 words answering the following question:

In a summary of the government's NHS Plan the Prime Minister cited partnership as a challenge facing the NHS.

a Explain the concept of Health Improvement Programmes.

b Give examples of partnership in health and social care.

MODEL ANSWER

Introduction

In this essay there are the following aims. An exposition will be given of the difficulties of having 'partnership' within the NHS. This account will be based upon the complex history of the NHS citing social, economic and political reasons as to why it is difficult to achieve partnership. After this general introduction to the issues inherent in the question there will be a description of the aims of 'Health Improvement Programmes' and a discussion of examples of partnership within health, education and social care.

The NHS which came into being in 1948 was established by the National Health Service Act of 1946. In 1948 its initial cost was £433 million (Moore, 2002, p35). It was introduced as a result of William Beveridge's attempt to turn Britain into a 'New Jerusalem', a place where social evils such as 'disease, idleness, squalor, ignorance and want' would be replaced by a kind and compassionate society. As Britain was recovering from the Second World War, Beveridge's ideals were of enormous appeal and a socialist Labour government introduced the welfare state (Harris, 2004, p52).

From this initial vision problems began to manifest themselves. Beveridge considered that the welfare state should look after the needs of its citizens from 'cradle to grave' but it soon became realised that such a partnership of people and state could never work. The Health Minister Aneurin Bevan resigned from his post as prescription charges were introduced. As each year passed, the NHS became more expensive and by the 1950s

MODEL ANSWER *continued*

Britain was financially bankrupt, a fact acknowledged by Harris (2004, p300). It may be argued that the NHS has become a complication to British society in that although it is considered as being important for society it is difficult to put into action.

This has led to the New Labour government of Tony Blair attempting to introduce what Giddens (2004) refers to as a 'third way' of policies that encourage cooperation. As health and social care costs have continued to grow, an emphasis is placed upon health and social care services working together. This point is illustrated through the establishment of health improvement programmes, primary care groups and the cooperation between private and statutory sectors.

(a) Explain the concept of Health Improvement Programmes

Health Improvement Programmes resulted following the 1997 White Paper 'The New NHS: Modern and Dependable'. Their main aim is to reduce inequalities in health. Large-scale health inequalities have resulted in health authorities being required to publicise what they are doing to improve health. The aims of Health Improvement Programmes include overcoming inequalities, modernising services, planning effectively and working with the voluntary sector and other organisations. It can be argued that local Health Improvement Programmes have benefits. These include greater sharing of resources among GPs, social workers, hospital consultants, pharmacists, and health visitors. This point is supported by Giddens (2004, p82).

The advantage of this approach is that the partnership being advocated will be a way of overcoming some of the practical difficulties experienced by the NHS. In a time of financial difficulty there is professional sharing and cooperation as well as an awareness of the need to supply detailed information about improving targets.

(b) Examples of partnership in health and social care

One of the most important examples of partnership in health and social care are Primary Care Groups. PCGs were introduced in 1999. They replaced the 'GP Fundholding' model. They differ from this approach to health care in that an emphasis is placed upon cooperation and consensus as opposed to competition. Whereas GP Fundholders acted more independently, PCGs comprise all local doctors serving a local population of 100,000 people. They meet together and plan the primary health requirements of the local population. An especially important way in which partnership results is that nurses are crucially involved in 'commissioning' or 'assessing' local needs.

A further example of partnership is the 'mixed economy of care'. As opposed to one sector of provision, the private, statutory, voluntary and informal sectors now work in partnership. This theme was recently emphasised by Tony Blair in his vision of an NHS that works alongside the private sector. It is also a theme developed at a recent conference by Durham County Council in which the relationship of social services with the statutory sector was emphasised as an important theme in local partnership.

Conclusion

In answering this question there has been reference made to the complex social, economic, and political factors that meant a 'free' welfare state became an impossible dream. Spiralling costs have meant that today's politicians have had to reconsider their approach to social policy. There is now a focus upon partnership and consensus management. This point is illustrated through the development of Health Improvement Programmes, PCGs and the mixed economy of care.

The 'Partnership Approach' to Social Policy and Early Years

The previous section of the chapter has outlined the origins of the idea of 'partnership'. New Labour are unable to return to the days of 'tax and spend'. To do so would risk a return to the economic problems that the UK experienced between 1945 and 1979. It is also not likely that New Labour will continue with Mrs Thatcher's social policies. Tony Blair was voted into power because he presented an alternative vision of social policy to the New Right. This means that the concept of 'partnership' is likely to continue to be an important component of social policy. A number of consequences impact upon Early Years. This section of the chapter considers three examples of how 'partnership' is put into practice within Early Years.

Every Child Matters

It can be argued that 'Every Child Matters' is one of the most influential aspects of social policy for Early Years. It attempts to address what Michelle Binfield (2006) refers to as 'an unwillingness to address a multiplicity of needs' (online) www.communitycare.co.uk. 'Every Child Matters' was published in 2004. The legislation resulted from the inquiry into the death of Victoria Climbié. 'Every Child Matters: Change for Children' represents the government's formal attempt to ensure that 'children aged 0 to 19' are 'protected'.

Key legislative features

Every Child Matters has five main aims. The legislation reveals the government's commitment to ensuring that every child in the UK is 'healthy, safe, enjoys life and achieves/makes a positive social contribution, and achieves economic well-being'. The key theme of the legislation is that the five main legislative aims can be achieved if 'integrated services for children' are ensured. This key point emphasises the importance of statutory, private, voluntary and informal children's services working together through partnership. The cooperation between 'local and central children's services' is also seen as being an integral component of 'effective children's services'. This process involves 'planning, implementing and assessing the effectiveness of children's services'.

Strengths and weaknesses of Every Child Matters

Every Child Matters is an example of a New Labour policy that attempts to improve the quality of life of children and families. It can be argued that this is in itself a worthwhile aim. Lumsden (2005) implies that the partnership approach with its emphasis on 'collaboration' does facilitate a model of 'coming together to solve problems' by providing integrated services. It can be argued that a weakness of Every Child Matters rests within its over ambitious aims. The BBC documentary 'When Satan Came to Town' (2006) reveals the difficulty of child protection because of the complex nature of child abuse cases. This may mean that it is impossible to ensure that every child in the UK is 'healthy, safe, enjoys life and achieves, makes a positive social contribution, and achieves economic well-being'.

REFLECTIVE TASK

Give a critical appraisal of 'Every Child Matters'.

FEEDBACK

It is difficult to be critical of any policy that represents an official commitment to child protection. Every Child Matters reveals that New Labour are officially acknowledging the importance of protecting children. This in itself is a laudable aim. It is also interesting to note that the five aims of Every Child Matters are similar to Beveridge's attempt to remove the five social evils ('disease, idleness, squalor, ignorance and want') from UK society. It can be argued that this philosophy of society is good in principle. The extent to which the approach will work in practice is, however, debatable. Alcock et al. (2000, p323) argue that New Labour's 'creation of a new welfare consensus is, at this stage, only a partial one'. This is because legislation alone does not bring an end to social problems such as 'child abuse'. It is challenging enough to ensure that all Early Years professionals know what 'Every Child Matters' represents, but even more challenging to put the legislation into effect within every Early Years context.

Mentoring

Alcock et al. (2000, p321) argue that a main feature of New Labour's approach to educational policy is to 'reinforce a greater role for parents'. This indicates that the traditional model of educational power has changed. As opposed to emphasising the autonomy of educational professionals, the focus is placed on a more equalitarian approach to education in which educators work alongside other professionals, children and families to enable what Alcock et al. (2000, p321) refer to as 'joined up solutions to joined up problems'. This has meant that 'mentoring' has become an important component of professional work.

In this context, mentoring can be understood as meaning 'the support given by one, (usually more experienced) person for the growth and learning of another' (Malderez,

2001, p57). From 2005 onwards, Ofsted have emphasised the importance of mentoring so that novices are 'nurtured' by more experienced 'experts'. This point is supported by the DFES research of 2006 that has investigated how the mentoring role within Early Years can be clarified so that Early Years mentoring can become more effective.

Strengths and weaknesses of mentoring

It can be argued that the 'joined up solutions' approach to 'joined up problems' within education is worthwhile. This point is supported by Brookes (2005, p43) who argues that the importance of mentoring was identified by Bell and Lancaster in 1805. In other words, an effective mentoring system has been identified as being an important component of education for many years. It can be argued that effective Early Years education is likely to benefit from applying 'the lessons of experience'. This means that there is nothing wrong with the principle of emphasising the importance of mentoring. What becomes more questionable is if mentoring is being recommended as an integral part of education yet there is no clear understanding of the model of mentoring that needs to be introduced. This is reported in the research of Ingleby and Hunt (2008). It appears to suggest that although mentoring is emphasised as being an important component of collaboration and partnership, the mechanisms for introducing and applying mentoring into education are unclear and ambiguous.

REFLECTIVE TASK

Give a critical appraisal of New Labour's 'mentoring' policy.

FEEDBACK

It can be argued that 'social policy' becomes 'ineffective' if it is nothing more than 'window-dressing'. In other words, if all the policy does is to 'look good on the outside' it will never meet complex needs. This may appear to be the case with 'mentoring'. It is a policy approach that 'makes sense on the outside'. It appears to be a 'good idea' until one asks questions about how mentoring is to be effectively implemented. The Ingleby and Hunt (2008) research raises five issues about the effectiveness of mentoring. These points are: the role of the mentor needs clarification; mentors need to be more aware of the educational aims of academic programmes; uncertainty is present over mentor training needs; mentor training is inconsistent; and professional boundaries between mentors and mentees are underdeveloped. This appears to suggest that the policy of mentoring can only become a part of 'collaboration' and 'partnership' if these questions are answered.

Multiple intelligences

Alcock et al. (2000, p321) argue that New Labour's partnership approach to society emphasises the importance of 'values of community, responsibility and social solidarity'. A consequence of this approach within education is to view educators and those being educated as 'working together'. This has had consequences for those who would have previously been unable to adjust to the demands of the educational system, for example children with 'challenging behaviour' and 'special educational needs'. The consequence of the partnership model is that as opposed to excluding children who cannot meet the demands of the education system, another approach is needed. This requires the education system to adapt to the needs of children who have previously been excluded.

A consequence of this approach is the implementation of learning strategies that are based on the ideas of Howard Gardner (1984, 1993, 2000). Gardner proposes that there are eight forms of intelligence. These are 'visual spatial', 'linguistic', 'logical mathematical', 'musical', 'bodily kinaesthetic', 'interpersonal', 'intrapersonal' and 'naturalistic' intelligence. Supporters of Gardner's ideas (for example Ofsted) argue that the traditional educational system is based on 'linguistic' and 'logical mathematical' intelligence. The argument runs that the educational system can be more inclusive if it acknowledges other categories of intelligence and in turn incorporates activities to develop these 'other' skills and abilities. This has led to the introduction of 'learning inventories' that attempt to identify the preferred learning style of groups of learners.

Strengths and weaknesses of 'multiple intelligences'

The attention that has been given to multiple intelligences can be seen as being positive if it leads to a more innovative curriculum for Early Years. Frank Coffield's (2004) research into learning styles does acknowledge that there are potential benefits in establishing learning inventories. This allows the possibility of tailoring teaching and learning in order to meet the needs of the learners. As opposed to making the curriculum an aspect of education that is 'followed by the learners', increased awareness of learning styles can allow for more innovative teaching and learning activities. If the group's learning preference is predominantly 'visual spatial' this can be used to justify 'visual spatial' learning activities. Coffield's (2004) research also gives a critique of learning styles. It is possible to ask 'why are there eight types of intelligence?' Why not nine or ten or more? Another critique of the implementation of learning inventories is that it adds on another layer of bureaucracy to the heavily bureaucratic teaching profession. This may mean that being aware of learning styles becomes more of an aspect of 'audit' to impress Ofsted inspectors than an innovative part of the educational curriculum.

REFLECTIVE TASK

Give a critical appraisal of New Labour's acceptance of 'multiple intelligences'.

Coffield's (2004) research appears to question the validity of the concept of 'multiple intelligences'. This argument can be developed to question the nature of the educational policy making process. Critics of educational policy making such as Lucas (2007) argue that too much education is 'standards driven'. This means that the educational process is not being fully acknowledged. The literal meaning of the word 'education' implies that the individual is enabled to see the world differently. This is less likely to happen if education is being 'standards driven'. If multiple intelligences are applied to education to impress Ofsted, this will not mean that they become an integral part of learning. They are instead akin to bureaucratic tasks that are standards-driven as opposed to being designed to educate individuals in the truest sense of the term. Coffield (2004) argues for a return to the notion of 'Platonic kings', in other words, for educationalists who are experts in practice and in turn able to shape educational policies. Perhaps this idea should be at the centre of future Early Years educational policies.

When you are next on the Internet do a word search for 'Every Child Matters', 'mentoring' and 'multiple intelligences'. Try to find out more information about these three aspects of New Labour policy. Make a note of how the three areas of policy affect your own Early Years setting.

C H A P T E R   S U M M A R Y

In this chapter we have seen that social policy is an important component of Early Years. Like psychology and sociology it is a discipline that has a rich heritage with complex socio-political and economic factors influencing the formation of differing social policies. The many complex aspects of UK society have influenced the social policies that are designed to regulate the social world. The chapter has explored three current themes within social policy that are influencing Early Years practice. The particular relevance of these policies for the Early Years context has been examined and a critical appraisal of each of the policies has been given. The concept of partnership and collaboration has been explored. These concepts can be understood if one looks at the wider context of social policy. It can be argued that the complex heritage of New Labour accounts for the focus on collaboration and partnership. It can also be claimed that all of these policy directions have fascinating implications for the Early Years context.

Self-assessment questions

1 What is the key policy theme of New Labour?

2 Name three influential areas of New Labour policy that are affecting the Early Years context.

3 Give an example strength and weakness of New Labour's approach to social policy.

Moving on

This chapter has introduced you to the idea of 'partnership' or 'collaboration' within social policy. Try to become familiar with this term. When you are thinking of doing research you might want to select an aspect of 'partnership' within Early Years as your research question. This will make your academic work directly relevant to the policies of New Labour.

Alcock, C., Payne, S., and Sullivan, M. (2000) *Introducing social policy*. Harlow: Prentice Hall.

BBC 'When Satan came to town', January 2006.

Binfield, M. (2006) 'Lack of duty acts as barrier to social care support for homeless people' 2 February 2006 (Online: www.communitycare.co.uk).

Blakemore, K. (2003) *Social policy: an introduction*. Buckingham: Open University Press.

Brookes, W. (2005) The graduate teacher programme in England: mentor training, quality assurance and the findings of inspection. *Journal of In-Service Education*, 31, 43–61.

Coffield, F.(2004) *Should we be using learning styles?* London: Learning and Skills Research Centre.

DFES (2006) Evaluating the EYSEFD: a qualitative experience of employers' and mentors' experiences, Research Report 752. London: Stationery Office.

Dicey, A. (1962) *Lectures on the relation between law and public opinion in England during the nineteenth century*. London: Palgrave Macmillan.

Gardner, H. (1984) *Frames of mind: the theory of multiple intelligence*. New York: Basic Books.

Gardner, H. (1993) *Multiple intelligences: the theory in practice*. New York: Basic Books.

Gardner, H. (2000) *Intelligence reframed: multiple intelligences for the 21st century*. New York: Basic Books.

Giddens, A. (2004) *The third way and its critics*. Cambridge: Polity Press.

Harris, B. (2004) *The origins of the British welfare state*. Basingstoke: Palgrave Macmillan.

Ingleby, E. and Hunt, J. (2008) The CPD needs of mentors in initial teacher training in England. *Journal of In-Service Education*, 34, 61–74.

Kesey, K. (1962) *One flew over the cuckoo's nest*. London: Picador.

Law, C. (1967) The growth of urban population in England and Wales, 1801–1911. *Transactions of the Institute of British Geographers*, 41, 125–143.

Lucas, N. (2007) The in-service training of adult literacy, numeracy, and English for speakers of other languages: the challenges of a 'standards led model'. *Journal of In-Service Education*, 33, 125–142.

Lumsden, E. (2005) Joined up thinking in practice: an exploration of professional collaboration. In Waller, T. *An introduction to early childhood: a multidisciplinary approach*. London: Paul Chapman.

Malderez, A (2001) New ELT professionals. English Teaching Professional, 19, 57–58.

Moore, S. (2005) *Social welfare alive*. Cheltenham: Nelson Thornes.

Plath, S. (1963) *The bell jar*. London: Faber and Faber.

Scull, A. (1982) *Museums of madness: the social organisation of insanity in nineteenth-century England*. Harmondsworth: Penguin.

Watson, A. (2004) Reconfiguring the public sphere: implications for analyses of educational policy. *British Journal of Educational Studies*, 52(3): 228–248.

Winter, J. (1986) *The great war and the British people*. Basingstoke: Palgrave Macmillan.

FURTHER READING

Alcock, C., Payne, S., and Sullivan, M. (2000) *Introducing social policy*. Harlow: Prentice Hall.
An excellent textbook in terms of detail and critical appraisal but the material is not always related to Early Years contexts.

Waller, T. (2005) *An introduction to early childhood: a multidisciplinary approach*. London: Paul Chapman.
An excellent textbook that is effectively organised and makes clear links to Early Years contexts.

4 Literacy and learning in Early Years

CHAPTER OBJECTIVES

After reading this chapter you should be able to:
- analyse how the child's personality develops over time;
- analyse how the child's linguistic ability develops.

The chapter develops your knowledge and understanding of literacy and learning within the Early Years context. This content is especially relevant to 'S2', 'S8', 'S11', 'S15' and 'S37' because these standards require you to reflect on how you can help to develop children's cognitive abilities within your own professional practice. Through applying knowledge about literacy and learning to the Early Years context it is possible to ensure that professional practice is as effective as possible. This is because reflecting on your professional role in relation to literacy and learning enables you to increase your understanding of what is meant by the term 'best practice' within this area of Early Years.

Introduction

He thought his happiness was complete when, as he meandered aimlessly along, suddenly he stood by the edge of a full-fed river. Never in his life had he seen a river before – this sleek, sinuous, full-bodied animal, chasing and chuckling, gripping things with a gurgle and leaving them with a laugh, to fling itself on fresh playmates that shook themselves free, and were caught and held again. All was a-shake and a-shiver – glints and gleams and sparkles, rustle and swirl, chatter and bubble.

Kenneth Grahame (1995, p20).

The saying goes that it is important to make sure that you never lose your sense of childish wonder about the world. It could be suggested that the quotation by Kenneth Grahame is steeped in wonder, the delightful fascination upon discovering that the world can be a wonderful place that is filled with creativity and vitality. Most people would probably endorse that a child should experience the world as a place of wonder so that they develop into adults who can look back on their childhood experiences with both affection and a 'wild imagination' (Ingleby, 2006, p135), namely to reword the saying: 'give me the child and you will see the person'. In other words there exists a critical link between the experiences of childhood and the characteristics of adulthood. This chapter looks at some of the contributions that have been made by social science in relation to understanding children and their development.

The work of Karin Crawford and Janet Walker (2003) is applied to the chapter. It is anticipated that its content is likely to be of particular interest to Early Years workers and other members of the multidisciplinary team who wish to work with children.

Perspectives explaining child development

Crawford and Walker (2003, p 18) draw attention to the number of perspectives that can be applied to understanding how children develop. These perspectives represent a combination of psychological, biological and sociological understandings of what influences child development. This section of the chapter introduces some of the key ideas within some of these perspectives. We have identified and explored the key psychological paradigms in Chapter 1 of the book. This section introduces what these perspectives say about child development in particular.

'Developmental psychology' is concerned with understanding how individuals develop over time in relation to their surroundings. It could be argued that all of the main psychological perspectives we discussed in Chapter 1 have some interest in child development. There follows a summary of what aspects of individual development are of interest to each of the perspectives. Before proceeding let us recall a working definition of each of the perspectives we looked at in Chapter 1.

REFLECTIVE TASK

Write out a working definition for behaviourism, humanism, psychodynamic theory, cognitive theory and biological psychology.

FEEDBACK

Behaviourism is particularly concerned with the impact that external environmental factors have on the mind.

Humanism theorises that each individual is unique and that the human mind understands the surrounding environment in an original way.

Psychodynamic theory proposes that the human mind is a combination of conscious and unconscious thoughts. Moreover the conscious mind is a small component of the wider unconscious mind.

Cognitive psychology is interested in what happens after a stimulus but before a reaction appears in the mind.

Biological psychology is interested in the impact that hormones and chromosomes have on thought processes.

Behaviourist explanations of child development

Behaviourist psychologists such as Skinner and social learning theorists such as Bandura are particularly interested in how cognitive processes are influenced by the surrounding environment. Crawford and Walker (2003, p 23) argue that Skinner considers child development as being 'the acquisition of behaviours which are learned through responses to experiences'. Of central importance to this explanation of child development is the idea that the individual child is not producing independent behaviour. In this theory, behaviour is viewed as being a response controlled by the rewards and punishments within the individual's environment. Albert Bandura is also interested in the ways in which the environment influences behaviour. As Crawford and Walker emphasise, Bandura considers 'cognition, or thought, to be a 'significant factor in the person's development'. This means that 'social learning theories consider the influence of values, beliefs, reasoning, self-determination, emotions and thought on the learning process'. All of these factors are crucially linked to the environment so it follows that what is understood to be a positive or negative environment produces thoughts within the child's mind that will be in turn positive or negative.

CASE STUDY

Joseph is six years old. He lives with his parents in a high-rise flat in a run down inner city area. Joseph's parents are both unemployed. His father is a heavy drinker and regularly abuses Joseph's mother physically when he comes in from the pub on a Friday night. Joseph's father has established a strong emotional bond with his son. He takes him out to the boxing club on Saturdays. Joseph's father used to be a keen boxer when he was younger and Joseph wants to be 'just like his dad' when he gets older.

REFLECTIVE TASK

What do you think would interest Skinner and Bandura about Joseph's personality development? How is this theory of child development relevant to Early Years?

FEEDBACK

Skinner and Bandura have both popularised the idea that child development is linked to external factors. Both psychologists would accept that 'Joseph's' thoughts are likely to be determined by his environment. Joseph lives with a father who is physically aggressive to his mother and moreover he has a strong emotional bond with his father. According to Bandura this means that Joseph is likely to 'model' or imitate his father's behaviour. The theory is of interest to Early Years because it suggests that in such circumstances it is entirely understandable for a child to be removed from an abusive household. What is also of interest is the complexity that this process is likely to cause, especially in

FEEDBACK continued

consideration of the relationship existing between the father and his son. It may be correct to remove a child from an abusive family environment but when there is such a close emotional bond between parent(s) and child, the intervening role of Early Years workers may be perceived in a very negative light.

Humanist explanations of child development

In Chapter 1 we identified that humanists such as Carl Rogers are interested in how individuals make sense of their environment. The environment is regarded as being important in that it is seen as being a major factor that shapes the individual's personality. It may also be argued that within the humanist perspective an emphasis is placed upon the environment influencing rather than determining personality. Whereas behaviourism may be interpreted as arguing that the individual is determined by the environment, humanism suggests that personality is shaped in conjunction with the environment. This means that humanists accept that the child develops by being influenced by its environment, but because the child's personality is unique it evolves in relation to its environmental circumstances. This argument is reflected in the following quotation from *On Becoming A Person*:

> *Experience is, for me, the highest authority. The touchstone of validity is my own experience. No other person's ideas, and none of my own ideas, are as authoritative as my experience. It is to experience that I must return again and again, to discover a closer approximation to truth as it is in the process of becoming in me. (Rogers, 1961, p23)*

In other words if we are to look to find the 'truth' of child development we must find out the nature of the child's experience of development. Rogers would argue that if the child has been unable to achieve their aspirations they are likely to be characterised by the 'would-should dilemma' outlined in Chapter 1. This will produce feelings of anxiety and impede personality development. Conversely if the child interacts with the environment in a positive manner and its aspirations are realised, the result is likely to be a balanced 'anxiety free' personality.

CASE STUDY

Alex is seven and is anxious about not being able to make friends in school. She is a quiet, withdrawn child and this persona is a reflection of the stress she has been under. Alex finds it difficult to cope with the school environment and she has been physically ill at the prospect of having to go to school. She makes little eye contact when she is in school and she speaks with an inaudible tone of voice. Alex is the youngest of a family of three. Her parents run a pub and Alex gets afraid of some of the customers who can become loud and aggressive. Alex does like art and music but her parents haven't encouraged this interest and this also seems to contribute to Alex's sense of anxiety.

How would humanists account for Alex's development? If you were working with Alex, what would you recommend she should do to improve her emotional state of mind?

Alex has a clear would/should dilemma. She wants to be good at music and art yet her parents do nothing to develop and support this interest. Rogers would argue that this accounts for Alex's personality problems. Her 'quiet and withdrawn persona' is a product of her low self-esteem. If you were working with Alex and you were applying client-centred therapy you would need to ensure that Alex communicated her wishes as assertively as possible. This might help to resolve Alex's would-should dilemma.

Psychodynamic explanations of child development

Psychodynamic psychology, as popularised by the work of Sigmund Freud proposes a dual model of the mind. The argument goes that the mind is a combination of conscious and unconscious thoughts. As we saw in Chapter 1, the theory proposes that whereas we are aware of conscious thoughts we are much less aware of unconscious thoughts. This may mean that we are unaware of why we behave in a particular way. Our unconscious thoughts are released and determine particular ways of behaving. As with humanism, psychodynamic theory acknowledges the importance that the environment has in influencing one's thoughts. It is argued that the manner in which a child progresses through the stages of development identified in Chapter 1 determines the thoughts that appear within the mind. This means that if the child experiences physical/emotional crises at any stage in their development the mind is likely to be adversely affected. As we saw in Chapter 1, it is important to remember that although psychodynamic theory can be interesting it is not necessarily accurate. Gross (1999, p917) adapts Popper's criticism of psychodynamic theory by saying that 'they are unfalsifiable and, therefore, unscientific'. In other words psychodynamic therapy can be applied but there needs to be the awareness that the therapy is not likely to offer every possible answer to every possible question.

Sarah has two children who are aged seven and five. Her husband has 'broken off' the relationship and left the family. Sarah thinks that her whole world had fallen apart since Philip told her they were 'finished'. Sarah has been unable to sleep and she has started to 'binge eat'. Sarah has been distressed and anxious and sought advice from an Early Years worker at a Sure Start centre. She had previously had a relationship with a boyfriend who had been a heavy drinker and had abused her verbally. Her husband seemed different. He seemed kind and Sarah had moved into his house and they have had two children together. Sarah was aware that other women found her husband attractive and at first she was pleased about this, but later worried that she did not have the ability to hold his attention. Sarah's mother had always warned her about the unreliability of men. Sarah is now worried that her emotional needs will affect the development of her two children.

REFLECTIVE TASK

How would a psychodynamic psychologist explain Sarah's personality?

How might these ideas be useful for Early Years workers who are working with children and families?

FEEDBACK

A psychodynamic psychologist would interpret Sarah's 'binge eating' as a sign that she has an oral fixation. This may be interpreted as suggesting that Sarah has experienced some kind of trauma between the ages of 0–1. In applying this perspective to understanding Sarah's behaviour it is also of interest that Sarah has an obvious tension in her relationships with men. This is indicative of a 'phallic fixation'. It suggests that there may have been a traumatic happening in Sarah's life between the ages of 3–6. A psychodynamic psychologist might suggest that Sarah has an unresolved 'Electra' complex. It could be proposed that the relationship between Sarah and her mother and father at the ages of 3–6 may have generated this Electra complex. It could also be suggested that this is an 'as if' argument! In other words it is 'as if' all of this has happened! Nonetheless for Early Years workers working with emotionally distressed children and families an explanation is offered for behaviour that may seem to be inexplicable. This in itself is useful for Early Years. Sarah's children are unlikely to have their learning needs supported by their mother unless her problems can be explained and helped. At the very least psychodynamic theory arouses debate and reflection about how and why the personality traits that affect children emerge and develop.

Cognitive explanations of child development

Cognitive psychologists such as Piaget and Vygotsky are interested in how the child's thinking processes develop over time. Both psychologists acknowledge that the environment has an important influence on how thinking processes evolve. According to Piaget and Vygotsky, children are likely to be impeded in their cognitive development if they do not have the positive environmental stimuli that are necessary for them to develop complex thinking processes. This means that both psychologists are interested in the factors that enable a child's mind to develop from birth onwards. The key question asked by both Piaget and Vygotsky is 'what is happening within the child's mind when it is receiving particular stimuli?' For Piaget the ideal is that the child reaches the stage of formal operations where it is capable of 'reversible' or complex problem solving (when a child can 'see in its head' that 3−1 is the same as 1+1). Vygotsky uses the term 'Zone of Proximal Development' (or ZPD) to describe when a child has reached its cognitive potential. Both cognitive states depend upon how the child interacts with the environment stimulating its cognitive processes.

CASE STUDY

Petra is seven. She has an older sister and a younger brother. Her father teaches in a primary school and her mother is a university lecturer. The family live in a pleasant house with a garden and a playroom. Petra has always been looked after by her parents. From an early age Petra's mother ensured that she followed a timetable of activities that was designed to stimulate her physical, intellectual, emotional and social development. Petra went to playgroup at two, nursery at three and began school at four. From an early age Petra seemed to be capable at English and maths. She could do 'sums in her head' by the age of six. Every evening Petra has 'mammy time' before bed where she works on English and maths activities with her parents. She has started to have piano lessons and her parents are hoping that Petra will eventually attend one of the few remaining traditional grammar schools in the locality. Petra says that when she grows up she wants to teach in a university 'just like mammy does'.

REFLECTIVE TASK

What would interest Piaget and Vygotsky about Petra's development? What is significant for Early Years practice about Petra's development?

FEEDBACK

Piaget would claim that Petra is well on the way to reaching formal operations and that she should be capable of reversible thought by the age of eleven. She is good at maths and English and she will eventually sit the 11+, an examination that is designed to test 'reversible thinking processes'. It could be argued that Petra's thought processes have developed because of the stimulation offered by her surrounding environment. Her thought processes have been nurtured from an early age. Vygotsky would be interested in the 'scaffold' of people supporting Petra's development. Her parents are both involved in teaching and have socialised with her during what they call 'mammy time' to make

English and maths a part of her world. This would propel Petra towards reaching her 'ZPD' (to use Vygotsky's term). It can be argued that what becomes significant for Early Years practice is the impact that a child's environment has on their cognitive development. It is true to say that in the case of Petra, she also needs to be in possession of the innate cognitive ability to respond to her environmental stimuli. With the exception of genetic engineering there is little that can be done to influence this capability but it is apparent that a positive nurturing, learning environment can be created and that this is a responsibility that Early Years workers must be aware of.

Biological psychological explanations of child development

Psychologists such as Gerald Davison *et al.*, apply a biological basis to their work. Davison, Neale and Kring (2003) propose that blood, injury and injection phobias are crucially linked to family background. This means that if someone has this specific phobia there is a 64 per cent chance a blood relative will also have the condition. In other words biological psychologists are interested in the relationship that exists between the thoughts within the child's mind and the individual's hormonal and chromosomal characteristics. These biological components are considered to be the critical factors in determining a child's thought processes. This means that biological psychologists are likely to explain sensory impairments, learning disabilities and language development deficits by identifying genetic, chromosomal and hormonal causative factors.

CASE STUDY

Bruce was surgically castrated as a baby boy. His gender was changed through biological and social processes. He was renamed Brenda and brought up as a girl. Through plastic surgery he was physically turned into a female. At puberty he was given female hormones in order to assist the process of gender change.

REFLECTIVE TASK

What would interest biological psychologists about Bruce's development? What might be significant for Early Years about the above case study?

FEEDBACK

Those applying biological perspectives such as Milton Diamond would be interested in the extent to which Bruce's biological maleness could be engineered into femaleness. If one accepts that identity is on the whole determined by genetic inheritance it can be argued that even with surgery, hormonal injections and socialisation, one cannot change what has been biologically determined. If this theory of child development is accepted (and there is increasing evidence to suggest that identity is linked to biological factors, for example Toates (2000)) Early Years workers need to be aware that child development is critically influenced by genetic inheritance and hormonal development.

The development of personality

Crawford and Walker (2003, p30) emphasise that personality 'development is influenced by and the product of a number of different and interrelated processes or systems'. This means that if Early Years workers are to gain an accurate understanding of the child's personality it is important to have some knowledge about what is referred to as the 'whole child'. This section of the chapter discusses some of the key factors that influence the development of the child's personality.

REFLECTIVE TASK

Think about your own personality. What would you say are the critical factors that have shaped your personality?

FEEDBACK

Upon being asked this question, many people immediately think that their parents have had an enormous impact upon their personality. How many times do we hear it said that 'she's just like her mother' or 'he's just like his dad!' We often associate our personality with our physical characteristics and we frequently assume that these characteristics have come from our parents. Moreover we may think that our level of kindness or the extent of our lack of kindness is a product of the traits that we have inherited from our parents. We may also think of how our family background, our relationships, our school and our peers have influenced our personality.

Critical influences on personality

Although a child's personality emerges over time it is important to acknowledge that the processes begin prior to birth. Crawford and Walker (2003, p 35) emphasise the importance of needing to understand the relationship between 'structural inequalities such as poverty' and the impact that these factors have upon the development of the unborn child. In other words, the mother's nutritional intake affects the growing foetus and this in turn has an impact upon the child's personality.

Once the child has been born, the first two years of life are acknowledged as being especially important (Crawford and Walker, 2003, p36). Psychologists such as Piaget have acknowledged that babies are born with a number of innate reflexes but it is important to emphasise that many aspects of personality are learned as the child interacts with its environment. The environment is an important factor influencing the formation of the child's personality but Crawford and Walker (2003, p37) emphasise the importance of understanding that a complex range of variables affect the child's personality from the ages of two to six. These factors include 'the child's genes, their temperament, their emotional and social development, the impact of the family, the context in which the family live and the culture in which the child grows up.'

Psychologists interested in child development have drawn attention to the importance of the relationship of 'attachment' between a child and its parents. The concept of 'attachment' has been popularised by John Bowlby (1953, 1969, 1973, 1988). It refers to the idea that mothers and children have an instinctive need for physical and emotional closeness within the early life of the child. Bowlby has referred to the separation of a child from its mother as an occurrence of 'maternal deprivation'. The consequences of this occurrence are regarded as leading to 'delinquent behaviour' and 'mental health issues'. Indeed Crawford and Walker (2003, p44) refer to the 'affectionless psychopathy' that results if the child perceives that they have lost their 'mother's love'.

Bowlby's work has not been without criticism. It could be argued that although a child may need to form an 'attachment' it does not necessarily mean that it has to make this attachment with its mother. This means that Bowlby may have focused too much on the child-mother relationship to the detriment of relationships with the child's father and its siblings. Another difficulty that has been commented on by Rutter (1981) is that in emphasising the importance of the mother's emotional warmth, other factors such as chronic lack of basic needs, and stimulation through play may have been neglected.

Nonetheless, it can be argued that despite these difficulties, attachment theory is of importance to Early Years. Crawford and Walker (2003, p46) emphasise that we need to be aware of as many factors as possible in relation to 'the nature, form and development of relationships' and one of these factors is indeed the extent to which the child experiences relationships of attachment.

As a child moves into 'middle childhood' (between the ages of five to twelve) it is likely to experience 'qualitatively different' physical, intellectual, emotional and social experiences (Crawford and Walker, 2003, p54). This is an important phase for the development of the child's personality because middle childhood may reinforce the experiences of early childhood. In Chapter 1 we identified that Freud regarded middle childhood as being a time of 'latency' with an emphasis being placed upon the development of social and intellectual skills. In relation to this point, the above authors (2003, p56) make reference to the work of Erik Erikson who refers to the ages of six to twelve as being a time during which the child reconciles feelings of 'industry' (or competence) in relation to feelings of 'inferiority'. In other words it is important for the child to be able to develop new intellectual and social skills such as reading, writing and the formation of friendships. Erikson also argues that it is particularly important that the child is supported at this stage of its life so that it does not develop a sense of inferiority or incompetence. If this happens, it may mean that the child's 'damaged personality' restricts its development into adolescence and adulthood.

How might Bowlby's attachment theory and Erikson's 'industry/inferiority' theory explain behavioural problems?

Challenging behaviour can be explained in a number of different ways. The cause may rest with the individual or it may be down to a number of complex occurrences that combine together and produce a series of challenging behaviours. It may be argued that if a child is overly insecure because of a lack of 'child attachment', this feeling may result in challenging behaviour. In other words it is the experience of insecurity that produces the challenging behaviour. The child may become overly aggressive in order to release 'pent-up feelings' or its personality may become increasingly introspective. It may also be the case that if a child develops particularly strong feelings of inferiority this can be expressed in a number of challenging ways. The child may become overly reclusive or develop 'self-destructive' behaviour such as 'self-harming' with the root of this behaviour being the sense of inferiority experienced and reinforced in middle childhood.

The development of thought processes

In outlining the development of the child's cognitive processes Jean Piaget and Lev Vygotsky have similarities and differences. The extent of their differences and similarities is open to debate. They are both cognitive psychologists interested in how the child's thought processes develop. The extent to which they acknowledge the influence of environmental factors on thinking processes is again open to debate. Whereas Piaget has been accused of being perceived as focusing on 'inner thought processes' Vygotsky is understood as placing an emphasis on 'potential' and the environmental factors that lead to this potential (Malim and Birch, 1998). This may be argued as being a significant difference between these two cognitive psychologists.

Piaget's theory of cognitive development

Piaget sees the intellect in terms of 'schemata' and 'operations'. Schemata are understood as being internal representations or 'cognitive plans' existing in the mind. According to Piaget a baby is in possession of a number of schemata, for example a 'looking schema', a 'grasping schema' and a 'sucking schema'. In other words its instinctive behaviour has a cognitive origin.

Piaget argues that these basic schemata are different to 'operations' or 'higher mental structures'. As outlined earlier, these cognitive processes have the characteristic of 'reversibility'. In other words they are more complicated mental processes. For Piaget, this kind of thinking is not acquired until middle childhood.

REFLECTIVE TASK

In Chapter 1 we identified that Piaget proposes that there are a number of stages of intellectual development. Write out these stages of cognitive development and give an outline of how the main characteristics of each stage of development relate to your knowledge of children.

FEEDBACK

Stage 1: sensorimotor stage (birth to two)
The child experiences the world through immediate perceptions. The phrase 'out of sight out of mind' applies. This means that thinking is dominated by the 'here and now'.

Stage 2: preoperational stage (two to seven)
As the child's linguistic ability improves it is capable of 'symbolic' thought. This means that the child can use words to refer to people and objects. This more developed thought is limited by 'egocentrism' and 'centration'. Egocentrism means that the child is unable to see the world from any other point of view but their own understanding of it. Centration means seeing one feature but ignoring the wider reality. In Chapter 1 we said that a child might think that a ton of lead is heavier than a ton of feathers, because the child has only thought of the objects as lead and feathers and not realised that both weigh a ton!

Stage 3: concrete operations (seven to eleven)
Piaget argues that at this stage of cognitive development the child begins to solve more complex problems. This provides the ability to 'decentrate'. It means that the child becomes less egocentric and is more capable of seeing the viewpoint of others. This stage of cognitive development is called 'concrete operations' because the child still needs to use practical objects in order to solve problems. A question such as 'Joan is taller than Susan; Joan is smaller than Mary; Susan is smaller than Mary; who is the smallest?' will pose difficulties for the child at this stage of cognitive development unless there is access to a pen and paper to solve the problem (it may pose problems with adults as well as children!).

Stage 4: formal operations (eleven+)
Piaget argues that 'formal operations' marks the beginning of abstract thinking. Problems can be tested in the mind and more complex ideas can be formed.

Vygotsky's idea of cognitive development

It can be argued that Lev Vygotsky differs from Piaget in that he is understood as placing a particular emphasis upon the importance of the role of other knowledgeable people in cognitive development. Thought processes should not be portrayed as being confined to the mind (and it could be argued that this is the impression one might get of Piaget's work even if this was not his intention). Vygotsky argues that the developing child forms a framework or 'scaffold' of influential peers who have a fundamental bearing on the child's cognitive development. It is this influence of others that is considered to be essential in forming individual cognitive concepts and problem solving skills.

Vygotsky also emphasises the importance of linguistic development in solving problems. It is argued that it is through talking about problems that individuals organise perceptions with three elements considered to be especially important:

- action: the ways in which individuals respond to problems;
- language: the ways in which individuals talk about problems;
- social settings: the places in which individuals are able to develop their problem solving skills.

We have referred to the ZPD (or Zone of Proximal Development) earlier and this is an important concept within Vygotsky's account of cognitive development. The ZPD is regarded as being the area between actual development and potential development. It is argued that the individual's potential development can be realised through positive interaction with others. As an example, a musically gifted child who teaches him/herself to play the piano will cross the ZPD into potential development with the help of piano lessons from an influential music teacher.

REFLECTIVE TASK

How might Piaget and Vygotsky's account of cognitive development be useful for Early Years workers?

FEEDBACK

It can be argued that if Piaget and Vygotsky's work is combined it offers a powerful explanation of the child's cognitive development. This account is particularly useful for Early Years practitioners who are working with children in a role that is designed to help the child's physical, intellectual, emotional and social development. Both psychologists emphasise that cognitive development depends upon how a child interacts with its environment. Through providing appropriate developmental activities the child's cognitive processes ought to develop accordingly. Through their explanation of how the child's thought processes develop, Piaget and Vygotsky offer guidelines that may be used to structure developmental activities. As an example, two-year-old children often enjoy making lines of objects such as cars. Piaget would argue that this schema needs to be nurtured and developed through play so that the child's mind can develop further schemata. Early Years workers who are involved with structured play with children can use these theories to aid the child's development. As well as making lines of objects, the child's mind can be stimulated through varying this activity (for example making objects appear and disappear and threading beads on a piece of string). These activities enable the child to develop its cognitive schemata. Vygotsky's work is important because it draws attention to the critical impact that an individual's social circle has in developing the mind. This means that it is important for Early Years workers to be aware of the link that exists between the child's cognitive development in relation to the influence of their peer group.

The development of language

In the previous sections of this chapter we have seen that the environment plays a particularly important role in the development of the child's personality and thought processes. It can also be argued that the child's environment has a critical bearing on its linguistic ability.

This point is emphasised by Bernstein (1961). Bernstein argues that there are two important forms of speech pattern, an 'elaborated code' and a 'restricted code'. Whereas 'restricted code' refers to the limited use of language, 'elaborated code' refers to using words in a creative and original way. For Bernstein, restricted code is characterised by 'basic linguistic conversation' exemplified by simple 'yes' and 'no' statements, closed questions, alongside the limited use of adjectives. Meaning comes more from tone, gesture, and other non-verbal/vocal forms of communication. 'Blunt' phrases are used and although the words used in the phrase are restricted, their intonation gives them a particular force.

In contrast to restricted code, elaborated code refers to more complicated uses of language. There is the occurrence of detail and images. This leads to the use of metaphor within conversations so that word-games result. The Kenneth Grahame quotation at the start of the chapter is a good example of what Bernstein means by elaborated code. It is 'rich text' that is overflowing with images and alliteration.

Bernstein argues that the type of language used by the child depends upon the type of environment they experience. In other words if the child's parents use restricted code, the child's conversation will in turn be characterised by restricted code. Likewise a child socialised into a family who use elaborated code will also use elaborated code.

Bernstein's emphasis on the link between socio-environmental factors is also at the heart of Piaget and Vygotsky's account of the child's linguistic development. The difference between the two theorists is neatly summarised by Richard Gross.

Piaget's view on language and thought can be summarised as claiming that language depends upon stages of cognitive development. Vygotsky argues that language and thought begin as separate but then come together when the child is about two years old. The significance of this is that by 1962 Piaget had come to accept this view (Gross, 1992, p373).

It can be argued that once more it is important to view Piaget and Vygotsky as complementing each other. According to Piaget, language begins as 'autistic' speech. This means that between the ages of two and seven, language directed at the self and at others cannot be distinguished.

Piaget argues that as the child's problem solving skills develop, autistic speech is replaced with 'egocentric' speech. Piaget proposes that this type of speech develops around the age of seven. It can be interpreted as meaning that language is used as a way of giving a running commentary on what the child is doing as it tries to make sense of its world. The final stage of linguistic development is 'socialised speech' where the child uses language in many varied complex ways.

Vygotsky's account of speech development in children can be used to complement Piaget's work. The theory claims that that until the age of two there are 'prelinguistic thoughts' and 'preintellectual language'. The former are initial perceptions and images. The latter are cries and babbles. The argument runs that when the child is two years old, both of these areas overlap resulting in verbal thought and rational speech. Vygotsky follows Piaget's argument by then claiming that whereas speech is initially egocentric it then develops into socialised speech. This theory of speech development is summarised in the subsequent illustration:

A number of debates exist in relation to the development of the child's developing linguistic ability. Plunkett (1981) argues that a central issue is the discussion that surrounds the extent to which grammar is a 'cognitive function'. This argument draws on Chomsky's (1972) argument that children learn to speak because of the possession of a 'Language Acquisition Device'. This cognitive function is considered to be an innate capability. Skinner (1957) adopts a different approach by claiming that speech is an

Prelinguistic thoughts (0–2)

Preintellectual language (0–2)

Language is produced when both unite

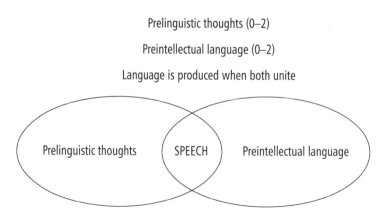

Figure 4.1 Children's linguistic development

example of social conditioning. It could be argued that the two approaches should not necessarily be seen as unworkable opposites. In other words, linguistic ability may be an innate human cognitive trait, but its development is also influenced by the social factors that are emphasised by Bernstein and Skinner. This produces the basis of the holistic approach to therapy referred to in Chapter 1.

REFLECTIVE TASK

How might the contribution of Piaget, Vygotsky, Chomsky, Skinner and Bernstein to understanding the child's linguistic development be of use to an Early Years practitioner?

FEEDBACK

Piaget and Vygotsky both draw attention to the stages of linguistic development within children. It may seem to be an obvious point but it is important to pay attention to the words that are used when we communicate with children. Both Piaget and Vygotsky acknowledge that 'socialised' adult speech takes time to develop. An Early Years worker working with children needs to acknowledge this idea so that speech can be used in a developmental manner.

It can be argued that Chomsky's idea of a 'Language Acquisition Device' implies that children have an innate propensity for using words. This means that in helping the intellectual, emotional and social development of the child it is important to incorporate 'word activities' into care plans whenever possible.

The work of Skinner and Bernstein is of importance to Early Years because it draws attention to the social issues within the child's linguistic development. This means that words can be used to create, develop and nurture social relationships. In order to develop best practice it is important for Early Years workers to be able to influence the professional relationship as positively as possible by considering the words being used to communicate this relationship. This may mean that it becomes important for Early Years workers to spend time aiding and assisting linguistic development. Koprowska's (2005) work in relation to communication skills might be applied to the Early Years context. Koprowska argues that if you have a raised awareness of how to develop children's linguistic ability, you are able to make a positive contribution to the child's cognitive development.

The importance of nature and nurture

This final section of the chapter appraises whether child development is a consequence of nature or nurture. This debate has been of interest to social scientists for a number of years. From the popularity of social learning perspectives through the 1960s, 1970s and 1980s to the contemporary critique offered by biological psychology there is a recurring interest in the link between child development and the influence of nature and nurture.

Biological perspective versus social perspective

We have already identified that the central idea of biological psychology is that genes and hormones shape our thought processes. Likewise the factors influencing the child's personality development are in turn reduced to genes, hormones and chemical reactions occurring in the mind and body. This means that the child's personality is attributed to internal traits. Malim and Birch (1998, p145) summarise the biological approach by saying that it 'studies the relationship between physiological and psychological make-up and the interactive influence of one on the other'.

In contrast to biological psychology, social perspectives on personality development adopt a similar argument to the behaviourists by arguing that the personality is a product of the social environment. One of the most influential studies to have popularised this perspective was carried out by the anthropologist Margaret Mead. Mead studied three social groups in New Guinea in the 1930s arguing that gender roles were cultural constructions. This is because each social group's expression of male and female identity depended upon shared understandings of what was believed to be appropriate male and female behaviour. Whereas the 'Arapesh' were characterised by non-aggressive affectionate characteristics in both sexes, the 'Mundugumor' were typified by males and females behaving in a 'masculine' aggressive and assertive way. In contrast, the 'Tchambuli' witnessed females being assertive and aggressive and males being gentle, passive and non-assertive. Mead's work appears to support the argument that personality development depends upon social factors. In other words we may be a physical product of chromosomes and hormones but social forces determine the development of the child's personality.

Appraising the argument

As opposed to seeing the child's personality as being a product of either nature or nurture it can be argued that it is more acceptable to propose that any personality is a complex product of both biological and social factors. This avoids reducing the complex components of an individual's personality to a set of 'either/or' variables. This is the central idea of Robert Winston's (2003) work that utilises the developments within genetic science alongside acknowledging the importance of social factors in shaping one's personality. It can also be argued that it is important to 'think outside the box' in order to try to become a 'paradigm shaker'. It is true that the traditional psychological debates have been interpreted as emanating from influential paradigms and that this influence has waxed and waned according to who has been associated with the paradigm. Nonetheless it can also be argued that if the debate is to move forward in understanding children's learning and linguistic development, it is important to combine ideas from various perspectives so that a holistic awareness of child development may be achieved.

PRACTICAL TASK

Using the Internet try to identify articles that are attempting to apply holistic approaches to child development. You might begin by going to a search engine and doing a search under 'holistic approaches to understanding child development'.

C H A P T E R   S U M M A R Y

This chapter has discussed some of the factors that influence children's learning and linguistic development. Each of the main perspectives identified in Chapter 1 has been considered in relation to this theme. In understanding how a child's thought processes and linguistic ability develops over time it can be argued that it is important to apply a holistic approach that utilises a breadth of psychological perspectives. This argument has been recommended in appraising whether a child's personality is a product of nature or nurture. It is too simplistic to adopt an 'either/or' approach in relation to this argument because the variables that determine personality can be many and varied. This can in turn assist the practice of Early Years workers because it suggests that the common-sense assumptions that often exist in relation to personality development may indeed be 'common' but they do not necessarily make 'sense'.

Self-assessment questions

1 Identify the main perspectives accounting for the development of the child's personality.

2 Analyse why Piaget and Vygotsky are claimed to have 'similarities and differences' in relation to the developing child's thought processes.

3 Appraise whether a child's personality is a product of either biological or social forces.

Moving on

The next chapter of the book considers the effect that 'different childhood experiences' have on child development. Think about how differing experiences of childhood can impact upon children's learning and linguistic development.

REFERENCES

Bernstein, B. (1961) Social class and linguistic development. In Halsey, A.H., Flaud, J. and Anderson, C.A. *Education economy and society*. London: Collier-Macmillan.

Bowlby, J. (1953*) Child care and the growth of love*. Harmondsworth: Penguin Books.

Bowlby, J. (1969) *Attachment and loss: vol. 1 attachment*. New York: Basic Books.

Bowlby, J. (1973) *Attachment and loss: vol. 2 separation anxiety and anger*. New York: Basic Books.

Bowlby, J. (1988*) A secure base: clinical application of attachment theory*. London: Routledge.

Chomsky, N. (1972) *Language and mind*. New York: Harcourt Brace Jovanovich.

Crawford, K. and Walker J. (2003) *Social work and human development*. Exeter: Learning Matters.

Davison, G., Neale, J. and Kring, A. (2003) *Abnormal psychology*. New York: Wiley.

Grahame, K. (1995) *Wind in the willows*. Hertford: Wordsworth Editions Limited.

Gross, R. (1992) *Psychology the science of mind and behaviour*, 1st edition. London: Hodder & Stoughton.

Gross, R. (1999) *Psychology the science of mind and behaviour*, 2nd edition. London: Hodder & Stoughton.

Gross, R. (2004) *Psychology the science of mind and behaviour*, 4th edition. London: Hodder & Stoughton.

Ingleby, E. (2006) Reinventing Melchizedek: interpretations of traditional religious texts. In Arweck, E. and Collins P., *Reading religion in text and context*. Aldershot: Ashgate.

Koprowska, J. (2005) *Communication and interpersonal skills in social work*. Exeter: Learning Matters.

Malim, T. and Birch, A. (1998) *Introductory psychology*. London: Macmillan.

Plunkett, K. (1981) Psycholinguistics, in Gilliam, B. *Psychology for today*. Sevenoaks: Hodder & Stoughton.

Rogers, C. (1961) *On becoming a person*. Boston: Houghton Mifflin.

Rutter, M. (1981) *Maternal deprivation reassessed*. Harmondsworth: Penguin.

Skinner, B.F. (1957) *Verbal behaviour*. New York: Appleton-Century-Crofts.

Toates, F. (2000) *Biological psychology: an integrative approach*. Upper Saddle River, NJ: Prentice-Hall.

Winston, R. (2003) *The human mind and how to make the most of it*. London: Bantam.

FURTHER READING

Malim, T. and Birch, A. (1998), *Introductory Psychology*. London: Palgrave Macmillan.
A clearly written text discussing child development in relation to Early Years.

5 Different childhoods in different cultures

CHAPTER OBJECTIVES

After reading this chapter you should be able to:
• recognise that UK family structure has changed over time;
• assess critically the impact of UK family breakdown.

The chapter examines the influence of the family on childhood. The central theme is that 'different cultures' (or 'social environments') produce different experiences of childhood. The chapter content is relevant to 'S3', 'S8', 'S17', 'S19', 'S25', 'S29', 'S30', 'S31', 'S32', and 'S38' because these standards require you to reflect on how child development is influenced by 'the family'.

Introduction

The chapter develops the sociological concepts that have been introduced in Chapter 2 by drawing on some of the work of social scientists researching 'the family'. The chapter begins by examining how different cultures influence the family. This means that there is not one 'universal family type'. As well as the 'nuclear family' of parents and children living together, there are 'extended families' characterised by relatives, parents and children living together. The chapter also explores the impact of history on family types in the UK. The 'nuclear family' has not always been in existence in this country. It is a family type that has evolved over time. The main theme of the chapter is that differing cultural characteristics make the experience of childhood 'different'. The impact of 'modern' UK culture on the family is examined in the penultimate section of the chapter. It can be argued that a characteristic of our modern UK culture is 'family breakdown' and this aspect of childhood is explored in the final section of the chapter.

Different cultures and different families

Haralambos and Holborn (1995, p317) cite George Peter Murdock's (1949) work in addressing the question 'is the family a universal social institution?' Murdock based his research on 250 societies. These families ranged from small 'hunter gatherer bands' to 'large-scale industrial societies', with the overwhelming conclusion being that every human society is characterised by 'the family'. Murdock understands the family to mean 'blood relations living together'. He uses his research to conclude that 'the family' is a 'universal social institution'.

FEEDBACK

The saying 'blood is thicker than water' is helpful in understanding why relatives are often perceived as being more important than 'friends'. Being 'related to someone' implies a biological link that can be the basis upon which a sense of 'obligation' is based. You might have defined the family as 'individuals related by blood who share a sense of duty towards each other'. Haralambos and Holborn (1995, p317) cite Murdock's (1949) definition of the family as a 'social group characterised by common residence, economic cooperation and reproduction' as a workable definition of 'the family'.

Murdock's (1949) work can be used to argue that the family is usually present in human societies. It can also be suggested that the type of family varies according to the social group's cultural characteristics. This variation in family type has interested social scientists for a number of years. The significance for Early Years is that the type of family appears to have an important influence on the experience of childhood.

Murdock (1949) considers the nuclear family to be especially important in human societies. His research identified that nuclear families were present in each of the 250 societies in his study. It can, however, be argued that despite the importance of the nuclear family, there are examples of other types of societies who have different family arrangements and this has an inevitable influence on the experience of childhood.

The Nayar experience of childhood

Kathleen Gough's (1962) work on the Nayar of Kerala in Southern India reveals that different understandings of the family exist in other cultures. These different understandings can have a profound impact upon childhood experiences. Gough's anthropological account of Nayar society reveals that before puberty, Nayar girls were ritually married to a 'suitable' Nayar man. Following this ritual marriage, the 'husband' did not live with his 'wife' and he was under no obligation to have any contact with her whatsoever. The only obligation that the wife had was to attend her husband's funeral and mourn his death.

Upon reaching puberty, a Nayar girl would take a number of visiting men or 'sandbanham' husbands. Nayar men would often be away from their villages as 'professional warriors'.

During this time they would visit villages and visit any number of Nayar women who had been ritually married. The 'sandbanham' husband would arrive at the home of one of his wives in the evening, have sexual intercourse with her, and leave before breakfast the next day. Gough reports that whereas men could have unlimited numbers of 'sandbanham' wives, women were limited to having no more than 12 visiting husbands.

The Nayar case reported by Kathleen Gough provides a very different experience of family life from most societies. The 'couple' were not in a conventional lifelong union. Moreover, 'sandbanham' husbands had no obligation towards the offspring of their wives. The 'father' of a child was expected to pay a fee of 'cloth and vegetables' to the midwife attending the birth, but the 'father' was not necessarily the biological father of the child. When a Nayar woman became pregnant, the only expectation was that 'someone' acknowledged that they were the child's father. The role of a father appears to be more of a social convention of 'acknowledgement' as a child's father had no social or financial obligations.

Gough also reveals that in Nayar society, husbands and wives did not form an economic union. Although husbands might give their wives gifts, there was no expectation for a husband to 'provide for his wife'. Moreover, Gough reports that if a husband did try to 'provide for his wife', this was frowned upon within Nayar society. The economic unit was made up of brothers, sisters, sisters' children and daughters' children. The leader of this social unit was the eldest male.

Nayar society is described as being 'matrilineal' by Haralambos and Holborn (1995, p318). This means that the family groupings were based on female biological relatives and marriage provided no role in establishing households, socialising children, or meeting economic needs. Sexual relations were socially sanctioned between couples who neither lived together nor cooperated together economically. Haralambos and Holborn (1995, p318) argue that the implications of Gough's work are that either Murdock's definition of the family is too narrow, or that the family is not universal.

REFLECTIVE TASK

What do you think the experience of childhood would be like for Nayar children? What do you think are the advantages and disadvantages of this experience of childhood compared to our culture?

FEEDBACK

Nayar children would have had very different relationships with their biological fathers compared to many children in our own society. The Nayar were a matrilineal society. This means that women were formally acknowledged as being of central importance to Nayar society. Nayar children would not have had close relationships with their biological fathers in comparison to the expectations of many children in UK society. If you think that children's growth and development is enhanced by a close emotional relationship with a biological father, you could argue that Nayar children experienced a less favourable family environment in comparison to the UK. It can also be argued that a close emotional relationship between a biological father and his children can often be an 'ideal' as opposed to a 'reality'. The experiences of many UK children can resemble those that have been so powerfully phrased by DH Lawrence (1956) in novels such as Sons and Lovers*. The harrowing scenes of domestic violence that Lawrence portrays are less likely to appear in Nayar society as the experience of childhood is not shaped by the nuclear family.*

The next section of the chapter continues to develop the theme that childhood experiences differ according to family type. As well as 'cultural differences', 'the family' has changed over time. This means that the experiences of childhood are linked to historical perspectives. The implication suggests that different times have been characterised by different types of family.

Different times and different families

As well as differing according to place, the family also differs according to 'time'. In other words, different times in history have been characterised by different forms of family. Haralambos and Holborn (1995, p334) make this point by arguing that pre-industrial societies can have very different family types compared to industrial societies.

Pre-industrial families

Anthropologists such as I.M. Lewis (1981) argue that kinship relationships are especially important within the social life of many pre-industrial societies. This is because individual families become part of wider kinship relationships and this means that the childhood experiences of family life can be contrasted with those experiences of children in industrial societies. Kinship groups are often linked by mutual rights and obligations. This sense of obligation is revealed by Haralambos and Holborn (1995, p335) who cite the reflection of a Pomo Indian of northern California to draw attention to the importance of the family for children in pre-industrial societies. As opposed to relying on 'the state', it is 'the family' who are considered as being 'all important'.

This means that instead of experiencing childhood within 'nuclear families', many pre-industrial children live in what Haralambos and Holborn (1995, p335) refer to as 'classic extended families'. These families are characterised by the 'extended family' being of particular importance. Haralambos and Holborn (1996, p335) argue that the traditional Irish patriarchal farming family that sees property passing down through male relatives is an example of this form of pre-industrial family. Within this family type, social and economic roles are amalgamated. The typical 'extended family' consists of a male head, his wife and children, his parents, and unmarried brothers and sisters. The family work together as a 'production unit' so that the family can maintain economic sustenance.

What do you think the experience of childhood would be like for children living in pre-industrial families? What do you think would be the advantages and disadvantages of this experience of childhood compared to the experience of childhood today in our culture?

FEEDBACK

You could argue that 'family breakdown' is a characteristic of family life in modern industrial societies. You could also argue that such family breakdown is less likely to be a characteristic of pre-industrial societies because families such as the Irish extended family relied on each other for economic sustenance. This means that the experience of childhood will be very different for children in these families. The choice of 'staying together' or 'separating' is a less likely option in this situation of economic dependence. In pre-industrial societies such as rural Ireland, children may not have had the material benefits that many children in industrial societies enjoy. It can also be argued that such children may not have experienced the 'pain of separation' that many children in industrial societies experience. As with all societies, there will be both positive and negative aspects of 'childhood experience'. It would appear to be the case that it is important to make sure that 'childhood' is not defined as 'absolutely better' or 'absolutely worse' according to time!

Was the typical pre-industrial society family 'extended'?

Peter Laslett (1972) has also contributed to our understanding of how 'time' influences family type. Laslett, a Cambridge historian, has popularised the nature of family size and composition in pre-industrial England. He found that from 1564 to 1821 there were only 10 per cent of households who had kin beyond the nuclear family living with them. This percentage is the same for England in 1966. Laslett also presents data from America to support his argument that pre-industrial societies are not necessarily characterised by 'extended families'. According to Laslett, the idea that a large extended family gave way to a nuclear family following industrialisation is a 'myth'. If this is true it might mean that there are more similarities in children's experiences in pre-industrial times than we might immediately assume.

Laslett developed his research by investigating pre-industrial family size in other countries. He arrived at the conclusion that the nuclear family was the typical family type in northern France, the Netherlands, Belgium, Scandanavia, parts of Italy and Germany. This family type contrasted with Eastern Europe, Russia and Japan where the extended family was more common. Laslett has used these findings to argue that the presence of the nuclear family was one of the key factors that led to Western Europe being the first area of the world to experience an 'industrial revolution'. This finding is supported by Berger (1983) who argues that the nuclear family facilitated 'modernity' because it encouraged patterns of thought that were conducive to industrial development. The argument runs that

FEEDBACK *continued*

nuclear families encourage individuals to be self-reliant and independent. These qualities are considered to be essential if 'industrial entrepreneurs' are to flourish.

Haralambos and Holborn (1996, p338) argue that Laslett's work is important because it 'exploded the myth' that the extended family was the typical family type for pre-industrial Britain. Haralambos and Holborn go on to argue that although Laslett's work does make a contribution to understanding childhood experiences, his conclusions need to be viewed with some caution. Michael Anderson (1980) has identified some contradictory evidence in Laslett's own research. Anderson argues that although the average household size may have been under five people, the majority of the population of pre-industrial Britain (53 per cent) lived in households of six or more people. Anderson also argues that in Sweden, extended families were very common and that family type between social groups in the UK evidenced considerable variation. As an example of this variation, Anderson discovered that 'gentry' and 'yeoman' farmers tended to have much larger households than the average. This is one of the reasons why Anderson is critical of the idea of the 'Western nuclear family'. He argues that it is more sensible to accept that pre-industrial Europe was characterised by 'family diversity' without any one type of family being predominant. If this is the case, it suggests that childhood experiences in pre-industrial times will vary according to what is accepted as being the 'ideal family type'. This reinforces a theme of this book, in other words that the diversity of human societies leads to differing and highly interesting interpretations of childhood.

REFLECTIVE TASK

Do you think that 'family type' is the most important factor influencing children's experience of childhood?

FEEDBACK

All of the chapters of the book emphasise the importance of the environment on child development. This is acknowledged by New Labour with their emphasis that 'Birth to Three Matters'. Four important aspects of children's development are regarded as being especially important within the 'policy' documentation. The importance of having a society with children who are 'strong' (or 'well-developed'); 'effective communicators'; 'good learners'; and 'healthy individuals' is emphasised as being a key goal for those working with children aged from 'birth to three'. You could argue that the 'platform' upon which these four aspects of development are built is 'the family'. Children are usually born into families and these familial experiences become crucial for children's development. This means that 'family type' or the sort of family environment experienced by the child can become critical to their development. A child's physical, intellectual, emotional and social development is likely to be determined by their familial environment. You might argue that 'genes, chromosomes, and hormones' are also critical factors in a child's development. In other words the 'biological nature' of a child is also of crucial importance to its development. It can be argued that it is difficult to identify which of these two factors is the most important for child development. You may choose to argue that 'biology' and 'family type' both have a critical role to play in how the child develops.

UK families: modern families in a modern culture

Investigating children's experiences of childhood in other cultures and through history reveals how different childhood can be through time and space. You could also argue that the experience of childhood in the UK today is also characterised by diversity. This point is made by Haralambos and Holborn (1995, p346). There is what Leach (1997) refers to as the 'cereal packet image' of the family. Leach uses this image to describe the 'typical family' being featured in some UK cereal advertisements. The image is of a happily married couple who have two children with the implication being that this type of family is somehow 'ideal'.

The idea that this 'cereal packet image' family is 'real' can be challenged if you consider some of the research that has been completed on the family. Haralambos and Holborn (1995, p347) make this point when they cite the research completed by Robert and Rhona Rapoport (1982). Their findings identified that only 24 per cent of families consisted of married couples, children and one 'breadwinner'. In other words, the UK has witnessed a decline in the number of households that are constituted of married couples and dependent children. Haralambos and Holborn (1995, p347) quantify this argument by stating that the percentage of UK households containing married couples and dependent children declined from 38 per cent in 1961 to 24 per cent in 1992. This point is supported by the increase of single person households. Haralambos and Holborn (1995, p347) record that the figure changed from 2.5 per cent in 1961 to 10.1 per cent in 1992. The Rapoports (1982) consider this trend to be similar in many other European countries. It is also a trend that has continued through to 2007. Social Trends (2007) reveals that almost a quarter of children in the UK were living in single parent families in 2006.

The Social Trends (2007) findings reveal other key statistics about the nature of family life. Of the 60.5 million people living in the UK in 2005, the proportion aged under 16 has fallen to 19 per cent. This figure can be put into perspective upon considering that in 1971, 25 per cent of the population were aged under 16. The statistics also show that the number of households in the UK has increased by 30 per cent since 1971, yet the actual population has only increased by 8 per cent. This suggests that children's experience of childhood will be very different in general compared with the preindustrial families that were exemplified in the previous sections of the chapter.

The Social Trends statistics reveal that nearly a quarter of UK children live in single parent families. What are the possible advantages and disadvantages of this experience of childhood?

You might think that there are no advantages for children living in single parent families. It may appear to be a less than ideal situation! You might have this view because of the general impression in our society that children's growth and development is enhanced by the nuclear family. It is, however, important to make sure that you don't over-generalise and think that 'all nuclear families are ideal and 'all single parent families are not ideal'. Children can be highly perceptive. In other words they 'sense' when they are loved and when they are not loved. If the children live in a nuclear family and the parents are constantly 'fighting' this can result in emotional difficulties for the children. They may feel unloved and this might have an adverse impact on their growth and development. In this situation it might actually be better for the children to be in a single parent environment.

The increase of UK single parent families

It is interesting to consider why there has been an increase in the number of children living in single parent families in the UK. Haralambos and Holborn (1995, p349) argue that the rise in single parent families is closely related to the increase in the number of parents being divorced. From 1971 to 1991 the proportion of single lone mothers who were divorced rose from 21 per cent to 43 per cent. Haralambos and Holborn (1995, p349) also cite that there was a rise in the percentage of single lone mothers. From 1971 to 1991 the figure changed from 16 per cent to 34 per cent. This suggests that the UK has become more accepting of diverse family forms. This point is made by David Morgan (1986) who argues that expectations of marriage have changed. Morgan also thinks that women have more opportunity to develop an independent life that does not depend on marriage or long-term cohabitation.

Haralambos and Holborn (1995, p350) suggest that another important factor to take into consideration is the decline in stigma that is attached to single parenthood. This is reflected in the way that phrases such as 'illegitimate children' and 'unmarried mothers' are less likely to be used today because of their negative implications. This appears to mean that the ways that many people think and talk about family life have changed quite considerably in recent years.

How this change in attitude towards families impacts upon the psychosocial welfare of children is a controversial and interesting question. Haralambos and Holborn (1995, p351) cite the work of McLanahan and Booth (1991) to propose that children may be harmed by single parenthood. The argument runs that children in single parent families have lower earnings and experience more poverty as adults. This research identified that children of 'mother-only' families are more likely to become lone parents themselves and that they are more likely to become 'delinquent' and engage in drug abuse.

Haralambos and Holborn (1995, p351) challenge the assumption that children who are brought up by one parent are 'worse off' than children who are raised in a nuclear family environment. The work of Cashmore (1989) is applied to argue that it is often preferable for children to live with one 'loving' parent as opposed to being with 'one caring and one uncaring parent'. It would appear that as with any experience of childhood there are variations according to the individuals concerned. There are some children who appear to cope more effectively with their circumstances than other children. This means that it is not correct to say that the experience of childhood will always be perfect in one particular family type.

CASE STUDY

The Nicholson family are one of the UK's many single parent families. Three children aged eight, six, and four live with their unemployed mother. The family members rely on state benefits for the majority of their income. The family's circumstances have had a significant impact on the children's development. There is never much money for the family to spend so this means that the food that is available is not of good quality. Mrs Nicholson finds it very hard to support the children's learning as she never has enough money to buy the books and other learning materials that are required to stimulate the children's intellectual development. The children realise that their circumstances are different from other families around them. This means that all of the children feel emotionally secure. Many other children are members of 'swimming clubs' and 'dancing clubs'. The Nicholson family do not have enough money to join these social clubs so the three children have to make their own entertainment.

REFLECTIVE TASK

How will the Nicholson children's physical, intellectual, emotional and social development be influenced by their circumstances?

FEEDBACK

Although the children in the case study may get on well with each other, their development is likely to be influenced by their circumstances. If the family budget is 'limited' this is likely to mean that the children won't have a particularly good diet. This will influence the children's physical well-being. The case study also suggests that the

FEEDBACK *continued*

family are unable to support the children's intellectual development as they do not have enough money to buy the learning materials that will reinforce the school's curriculum activities. The emotional insecurity and social isolation are also linked to their financial circumstances. This means that the Nicholson family may have a less positive experience of family life compared to other children in different circumstances.

The importance of ethnicity

Haralambos and Holborn (1995, p351) draw attention to the importance of ethnicity in contributing to UK family diversity. The main ethnic groups who have immigrated into the UK have tended to adapt their ideas of family life to UK circumstances. Haralambos and Holborn (1995, p351) go on to argue that the acceptance of cultural diversity within the UK has meant that family diversity is possible. It can also be argued that this in turn influences childhood experiences of family life.

The Social Trends (2007) statistics reveal differences in family type between different cultural groups. Whereas over 80 per cent of UK Indian dependent children live with married parents, only 30 per cent of Black Caribbean dependent children live with married parents. This appears to suggest that the importance of marriage varies with cultural beliefs. This also appears to contribute to different experience of childhood in the UK.

Haralambos and Holborn (1995, p353) refer to the work of Roger Ballard to reveal how changing cultural circumstances influence family life. Ballard (1990) has popularised how South Asian family life can change as a result of emigration to the UK. Whereas South Asian families are traditionally based around a man, his sons, and grandsons, migration to the UK can lead to an increasingly important economic role for women. This is in turn likely to impact upon the experiences of childhood as women become more associated with wage labour. Ballard suggests that families are more likely to be split into smaller domestic groupings as a result of these changing economic circumstances alongside the UK cultural expectation that 'extended families' are not the usual family type.

CASE STUDY

Benjamin is seven. His ethnic background is Afro-Caribbean and he lives with his mother and two elder brothers. Benjamin has never known his father. The only male role models that Benjamin has ever been close to are his two elder brothers. Benjamin has become emotionally close to his eldest brother and he has been visibly affected by his brother's recent arrest for possessing cannabis. Benjamin's mother and brothers cannot accept that possessing cannabis can be against the law as it is accepted as a cultural norm within the wider local community. Benjamin 'hero worships' his elder brother and at a recent community liaison event he refused to speak to the local police representatives. Benjamin's mother is anxious about what will happen to Benjamin in the future. She thinks that his childhood days should be the happiest of his life. It saddens her to think that at the age of seven he is already aware of community tensions.

How is Benjamin's cultural background influencing his experience of childhood?

You may think that too many UK children appear to 'grow-up' too quickly and lose their childhood at an early age. In the above case study, Benjamin's mother is anxious that the challenges of the modern world are already having a negative impact on Benjamin's experience of childhood. You could argue that childhood experiences should not be influenced negatively by 'differing cultural beliefs'. On the other hand you might also argue that unless all cultural groups follow the same legal system, social tensions and potential anarchy may result. In the case study it appears that Benjamin's cultural background is at odds with UK law. His experience of childhood is more influenced by his cultural background than by his identity as a UK citizen. This appears to be at the centre of the tensions that the family are experiencing.

Family breakdown

It can be argued that 'family breakdown' is becoming more apparent within UK society. Haralambos and Holborn (1995, p370) cite the decline in the popularity of marriage alongside the increasing occurrence of marital breakdown as evidence that the UK is witnessing an increased amount of family breakdown. It can also be argued that despite these two social trends, most people in the UK still live in families so it is important not to over-emphasise the importance of family breakdown.

The argument that there are 'threats to marriage' in the UK has been popularised for a number of years. Robert Chester (1985) drew attention to the decline in marriage rates among young adults in Western countries such as Sweden, Denmark, the UK, Germany and the USA. The statistics supporting this change in trends reveal that in 1971, one in 11 teenage women was married. By 1981 this had fallen to one in 24. Alongside this statistic, Haralambos and Holborn (1995, p370) cite that between 1981 and 1990 the marriage rate in the UK for all age groups fell from 7.1 per year per thousand of all the eligible population, to 6.8.

UK statistical data does appear to show that family trends have changed over the last three decades. Social Trends (2007) reveals that the percentage of people living in the UK in lone parent families with dependent children has risen from 3 per cent in 1971 to 7 per cent in 2005. These changing family trends are referred to by Joan Chandler (1991) in her research into UK 'cohabitation' or 'living together'. Chandler argues that the social convention to 'marry first and then have children' has lessened within the UK. This appears to be an important factor influencing UK family life. This will in turn have a significant impact on UK children's experience of childhood.

The Catholic Church view marriage as a 'sacrament', or 'sacred'. If many UK couples do not accept this interpretation of marriage how will this affect their children's experience of childhood?

FEEDBACK

It can be argued that as with many forms of social life, differing interpretations of 'right and wrong' have differing 'advantages and disadvantages'. To view marriage as a 'sacrament' and having a 'spiritual' quality can be a great advantage if this means that a couple love each other and consider their children to be a 'gift' or a 'blessing'. The advantage of this view can be seen in many UK Catholic families who appear to have a strong belief in the importance of marriage as a 'sacred sacrament'. This belief can appear to inform their loyalty and commitment to the family. It can also be argued that as long as this view of family life does not become intolerant of others who do not share the same belief it will make a positive contribution to UK social life.

PRACTICAL TASK

When you are next on the Internet, visit the UK Social Trends website. Try to find out more information about UK family trends affecting the experience of childhood from the Social Trends statistical data.

Marital breakdown

Haralambos and Holborn (1995, p370) argue that there are three main categories of marital breakdown. These are listed as 'divorce'; 'separation'; and 'empty-shell marriages'. Divorce can be defined as being 'legal separation' whereas 'separation' differs from divorce because there are not the same legal implications. 'Empty-shell marriage' is a term that is used to describe couples who are legally married but their marriage exists in name only.

The UK Social Trends statistics reveal that there has been a steady rise in divorce rates. The number of divorces occurring in Britain doubled between 1958 and 1969. Social Trends (2006) reveals that in 2004 the number of UK divorces was 167,100. This represents a fourth successive yearly rise.

This UK divorce rate is very high compared to other European countries. Haralmabos (1995, p372) records that only Denmark had a higher rate in 1990. Although it is relatively easy to quantify the number of divorces, it is more difficult to identify the number of instances of 'separation' and 'empty-shell marriages'. Haralambos and Holborn (1995, p372) propose that whereas the instance of UK separation has probably increased, the extent of empty-shell marriage has lessened. It can be argued that this is because of the changing attitude to relationships within the UK. This echoes Ingleby and Hunt's (2008) argument that the 'social discourse' or ways of talking about relationships have changed over time within the UK. This means that an emphasis is now placed upon the rights of the individual as opposed to emphasising the importance of 'society' and 'institutions'.

Nicky Hart (1976) explains marital breakdown by considering the 'value' that is given to marriage, the level of 'conflict' that exists between spouses and the degree of possibility of 'escaping' from marriage. This means that if marriage is not highly valued, if conflict levels are high within the marriage and if it is easy to 'escape' from marital ties, there is more possibility of the marriage 'failing'. All three factors do appear to have become a 'norm' within UK family life in general.

Divorce legislation

The changing attitude to divorce within the UK has been institutionalised by a number of changes in the law. These legal changes have made it easier to obtain a divorce settlement. Haralambos and Holborn (1995, p374) acknowledge that before 1857, a private act of parliament was required to obtain a divorce. This procedure was not possible for the majority of the population because it was so expensive.

Since 1857, divorce costs have fallen and the grounds for divorce have been widened. The 1971 Divorce Reform Act defined the grounds for divorce as 'the irretrievable breakdown of the marriage'. This has made divorce easier and helps to explain why there has been such a dramatic rise in the number of divorces in the UK since 1971.

Additional divorce legislation was also introduced at the end of 1984. This legislation reduced the period that a couple needed to be married before they could petition for divorce from three years to one. The legislation also made the 'behaviour of the married partners' the key influencing factor in deciding marriage settlements. This meant that if the behaviour of one partner was the key factor leading to the divorce, the other partner's 'liability' would be reduced in the subsequent divorce settlement.

REFLECTIVE TASK

Do you think that divorce rates will continue to rise in the UK? How do you think this will influence children's experiences of childhood?

FEEDBACK

If the Social Trends statistics are to be believed then it would appear to suggest that the number of divorces will continue to rise. Of course this might not mean that marriage is less popular. It might mean that there is more marriage if divorced people re-marry. The Social Trends statistics appear to support this argument. They reveal that the figure of 286,100 marriages in 2001 rose to 308,600 in 2003. Despite this statistic, it appears to be

FEEDBACK continued

the case that divorce is a pertinent UK social trend. This will have an impact on children's experience of childhood within the UK. We have already mentioned that within the UK concern has been expressed about children 'growing up too soon'. Perhaps this happens because of the lack of stability within many UK families? This might mean that the experience of childhood is negative and there is a wish to 'move on' to the adult world. If this is true it once again provides another different experience of childhood.

CHAPTER SUMMARY

In this chapter we have identified that there is not one universal type of family. We have identified that family type differs according to time and space. In other words, through history and through culture there are differing family types. The chapter has also revealed how UK families have been influenced by cultural trends. It would appear that one of the most important factors influencing UK families is the experience of 'family breakdown'. All of these factors have a tremendous influence on children's experience of childhood. It can be argued that one of the most fascinating aspects of applying social science to Early Years is witnessing the variety of children's experience within the known world. Children appear to engage with the world around them and interpret these experiences in a unique way. This means that the essence of studying children appears to rest in this diversity of experience. To be aware of this characteristic appears to be the best way of applying social science to Early Years.

Self-assessment questions

1 Is the 'nuclear family' a universal family type?

2 What are two important factors that appear to influence family form?

3 What is one of the key factors influencing UK children's experience of childhood today?

Moving on

This chapter has introduced you to the idea of how family type influences childhood experiences. You might want to think of developing some research ideas within this area of study in order to contribute to your continuing professional development.

REFERENCES

Anderson, M. (1980) *Approaches to the history of the western family 1500–1914*. London: Macmillan.

Ballard, R. (1990) Marriage and family. In Clarke, C. Peach, C and S Vertovec, S. (eds) *South Asians overseas*. Cambridge: Cambridge University Press.

Berger, P. (1983) *The war over the family*. London: Hutchinson.

Cashmore, E.E. (1989) *United Kingdom*? London: Unwin Hyman.

Chandler, J. (1991) *Women without husbands: an exploration of the margins of marriage*. London: Macmillan.

Chester, R. (1985) The rise of the neo-conventional family. *New Society*, 9 May, 1985.

Gough, K. (1962) Nayar: central Kerala. In Schneider, D. and Gough, K. (eds) *Matrilineal kinship*. Cambridge: Cambridge University Press.

Haralambos, M. and Holborn, M. (1995) *Sociology: themes and perspectives*. London: HarperCollins.

Hart, N. (1976) *When marriage ends: a study in status passage*. London: Tavistock Press.

Ingleby E. and Hunt, J. (2008) The CPD needs of mentors in initial teacher training in England. *Journal of In-Service Education*, 34, 61–74.

Lawrence, D.H. (1956) *Sons and lovers*. London: Heinemann.

Laslett, P. (1972) *Household and family in past time*. Cambridge: Cambridge University Press.

Leach, E. (1997) *A runaway world?* London: BBC Publications.

Lewis, I.M. (1981) *Social anthropology in perspective*. London: Penguin Books.

McLanahan, S. and Booth, K. (1991) *Contemporary families*. Minneapolis: National Council on Family Relations.

Morgan, D. (1986) Gender. In Burgess, R. (ed.) *Key variables in social investigation*. London: Routledge & Kegan Paul.

Murdock, G.P. (1949) *Social structure*. New York: Macmillan Press.

Rapoport, R. and R. (1982) *Families in Britain*. London: Routledge & Kegan Paul.

Social Trends (2007) *Social trends*. London: Palgrave Macmillan.

FURTHER READING

Haralambos, M. and Holborn, M. (1995) *Sociology: themes and perspectives*. London: HarperCollins.
A useful textbook in terms of clarity of content and analysis but the material is not always directly related to Early Years contexts.

Yeo, A. and Lovell, T. (2003) *Sociology for childhood studies*. London: Hodder & Stoughton.
An excellent textbook that is written in an accessible way and makes clear links in identifying how the family influences children's experiences of childhood.

6 Research methods for EYPS

Introduction

This chapter explores key aspects of the research process. The chapter identifies a number of key research models, the methods that can be applied within the research process and aspects of good practice that are especially important if effective research is to happen. The research process is outlined, analysed and critically appraised in order to investigate how research methods can be applied to Early Years. As with previous chapters, there are formative activities that reinforce learning in relation to the main aspects of the research process.

Defining research

REFLECTIVE TASK

What is your understanding of the word research?

FEEDBACK

Research is an important part of every academic discipline. The term means discovering new information about a subject. When we discover this new information it enables us to confirm or dispute whether previous understandings of academic matters still apply. We can say that there are two especially influential theories that have influenced research. These are the 'normative' and 'interpretive' models of research. The two theoretical perspectives provide opposing models of research. The normative perspective is scientific in its approach. This is because it recommends that the best way to gather research data is to adopt a scientific perspective in order to gather statistics and quantifiable data. In contrast, the interpretive perspective is non-scientific in its approach. Interpretive research attempts to gather the views and opinions of individuals in a non-statistical way. These narrative accounts are used to present individual interpretations of the social world. Both approaches to research are summarised in the following dictionary definition of research:

Diligent and systematic inquiry or investigation into a subject in order to revise facts, theories, applications.

Online dictionary

Research is important for Early Years practitioners because it provides the opportunity to revise and reinforce understandings of the Early Years context. This means that being aware of the research process enables you to increase your knowledge of the latest findings about the factors influencing children and families.

The research process

The research process is characterised by competing models of research. The previous section of the chapter refers to the normative and interpretive models of research. Both of these approaches have a distinctive philosophy of the research process. This means that the data gathering methods that are chosen are influenced by the underlying research philosophy. Whereas the normative approach to research emphasises the importance of 'scientific processes' the interpretive perspective is non-scientific in its outlook. This results in data-gathering methods that are concerned with gathering non-scientific or qualitative data.

Competing perspectives

As well as the normative and interpretive research perspectives, 'action research' is another influential research perspective. This research model emphasises the importance of researching professional practice so that the findings can be used to influence future work. This approach to research is often used within education so that the findings can be applied to improve professional practice. These research perspectives are described as being in competition because they have a conflicting understanding of the research process and how this process should be applied.

Research methods

Research methods refer to the data-collection processes that are applied by researchers. The data that is gathered is in general either 'quantitative' (or statistical) or 'qualitative' (or non-statistical). The research methods employed by the researcher are either 'primary' (or the immediate work of the researcher) or 'secondary' (in other words using the findings of other published researchers). The techniques used to gather this data can include questionnaires, interviews, observations, focus groups, case-studies and book-based research in 'learning resource centres'.

Validity

Validity refers to the acceptability of the research. There are accepted conventions followed by academic researchers, for example being aware of ethical issues. This means that it is important for researchers to be able to identify what is accepted as being 'good practice' within research. Research should not be used to harm others. There should always be consent and openness within any research project. If these principles are not apparent this can mean that the research is not valid or acceptable.

Four types of validity are 'face validity'; 'content validity'; 'empirical validity'; and 'predictive validity'.

Face validity
This aspect of validity asks whether the research methods within a research project measure what should be measured. For example, is the data that is gathered by an initial questionnaire used to generate semi-structured interviews or are the two processes unrelated? If the research methods are unrelated to each other the validity, or acceptability of the research can be questioned.

Content validity
Content validity relates to the theoretical content of the research process. Have key concepts been covered by the research? If they have, this means that the research is more likely to be valid. Research projects often have a 'literature review' section. This is one way of attempting to show that key concepts have been covered.

Empirical validity
This element of validity asks whether the research data supports the research question in a positive way. Does the data that has been gathered answer the research question in enough depth and detail? Has sufficient data been gathered or is there a need for more data gathering if the research question is to be answered comprehensively?

Predictive validity
This aspect of validity looks at whether or not accurate predictions for the future can be made as a result of the research. Have definite findings been obtained that give enough depth and substance to predict future developments for the research area?

Reliability

'Reliability' refers to the accuracy or otherwise of the research findings. The ideal is for the research to produce consistent findings. If the research is characterised by this consistency of findings over time this adds to the quality of the research process. Like validity, there are a number of different types of reliability within research.

Inter-observer reliability

This example of reliability refers to different researchers finding similar research findings. The discovery of this 'pattern' means that the research process has identified consistent findings.

Test-retest reliability

This form of reliability uses the same methodology to produce consistent findings on a number of occasions. Once more, it is the discovery of a 'pattern' within the research that means we can say that the research is reliable.

Inter-item reliability

This type of reliability means that different research methods are used in order to produce consistent findings. As an example, questionnaire data may be used to inform a semi-structured interview and a focus-group. If the findings from these research methods are consistent, this will add to the reliability of the research findings.

Triangulation

This term has been popularised by Norman Denzin and Y. Lincoln (2000). Triangulation means that the researcher uses at least three different ways of gathering research data. As an example, a researcher might use questionnaires, interviews and library research as the three sources of data. As long as the data has been gathered effectively and there is depth and detail of content, the subsequent theory is more likely to be valid and reliable. Like 'reliability' and 'validity', there are different ways of showing that you have triangulation of data.

Methodological triangulation

This type of triangulation is characterised by the researcher using many different but complementary research methods.

Data triangulation

This form of triangulation draws on many different but complementary sets of data.

Investigator triangulation

This form of triangulation uses the research findings of many different researchers.

Theory triangulation

This type of triangulation uses a number of different but relevant theories to interpret the research findings.

Research ethics

Researchers need to be aware of ethical good practice. Ethics refers to applying moral principles in order to ensure that the research subjects are never harmed by the research process. Opie (2004, p25) defines research ethics as 'the application of moral principles to prevent harming or wronging others, to promote the good, to be respectful and fair'. Ethics needs to be considered at all points of the study, from the design of the research question to interpreting the results, and presenting the findings.

Designing the research question
It is important to ask yourself what you want to know and why you want to research into your chosen topic. This is so that you can confirm that you have a justifiable interest in your area of research. If your research is in any way 'experimental' it is important to consider the implications for those involved. Opie (2004, pp25–26) emphasises the importance of asking yourself about the 'potential consequences' of the research.

Procedures for data collection
When you are gathering research data, it is important to ensure that you never ask your research participants anything that you would not want to be asked. It is also important to make sure that you never ask people to do anything that you would not want to be asked to do. Opie (2004, p27) considers that these two points are 'the acid test' of good practice within research.

Research relationships
It is important to remember that you have a moral responsibility to the people that you are working with. Make sure that you do not manipulate the research relationship to get 'good data'. It is also important to be aware of the power relationship that exists between you and the research subjects. Opie (2004, p29) draws attention to the powerful position that you can be in as a researcher and the powerless position that may be experienced by those being 'researched'.

Data interpretation and analysis
It is important to be aware of any theoretical frameworks or value systems that might influence your data interpretation and analysis. The research process can be complicated and it is important to acknowledge challenges in answering research questions as opposed to making the process appear 'neat' and 'uncomplicated'. Opie (2004, pp30–31) emphasises that protecting research subjects in written accounts is especially important if ethical principles are to be maintained.

Data dissemination
When you present your research findings it is important to ensure that your research participants' anonymity is protected. The most essential principle is for you to avoid harming anyone during the research process. Opie (2004, p32) recommends that researchers always have to consider whether 'the ends justify the means' during the research process.

The following table summarises the essential points of good practice that need to be remembered if good practice within research is to be maintained:

Table 6.1 'Remember' research ethics

Remain true to your data in order to maintain professional integrity.

Ensure the physical, social, psychological well-being of research participants is never adversely affected.

Make your research participants know how far they will be given anonymity and confidentiality.

Excessive covert or 'hidden' research violates the principles of informed consent.

Make no threats to confidentiality and anonymity of research data.

Be especially careful if your research subjects are vulnerable because of age, disability, physical and/or mental health.

Extra care is required if your research involves children. The consent of parent and child must be sought.

Research participants need to know that they have the right to refuse to participate.

From this initial discussion about the research process we can now explore the concept 'methodology'.

REFLECTIVE TASK

What do you think the word 'methodology' means?

FEEDBACK

The word 'methodology' sounds like the word 'method'. A way of explaining this word is to think about studying different ways of doing research. There are different research methods or ways of completing research. We have previously identified the difference between the 'normative' and 'interpretive' approaches to doing research. Whereas the normative approach places an emphasis on 'scientific' methods, the interpretive approach is 'non-scientific' in its emphasis. 'Methodology' is a word that means the study of methods of data collection. It is important to emphasise that as well as differing theoretical approaches to gathering data, there are a number of different research methods. These research methods gather quantitative (numerical) and/or qualitative (non-numerical) data. The sort of data that is gathered depends on the approach of the researcher. If you have a scientific approach to your research question you are likely to gather quantitative data. If you are non-scientific in your research approach you are likely to gather qualitative data. The methods that are used can include questionnaires, surveys, interviews, observation, focus-groups, experiments and library research. These research methods can be used in isolation or combined together to produce comprehensive research findings. The number of methods being used depends upon the nature of the research question and the specific research objectives.

We can now add more detail to our discussion of research perspectives and data-collection methods. This a way of setting the scene before we look at how the research process can be applied to Early Years practice and the role of the Early Years Professional in particular.

The research models

In the following table there is a summary of three influential models of research with a brief description of their key features.

Table 6.2 Research models

Research model	Key features
Normative	This perspective was popularised initially by David Hume in the eighteenth century. It emphasises the importance of 'scientific' approaches to understanding the world.
Interpretive	This school of thought has been popularised by Edmund Husserl. It emphasises the importance of non-scientific approaches to the research process.
Action research	This model of research has been popularised by Kurt Lewin since the 1940s. It emphasises the importance of researching professional practice. The objective of the research is to improve future professional practice.

These models of research are especially useful to you as an EYP because of the influence they have had in shaping the research process. As an EYP you will need to influence practitioners by drawing attention to examples of good professional practice. Knowledge and awareness of research about Early Years will help you to develop as a professional. As with the psychological and sociological perspectives we have looked at thus far, the origins of the ideas in these models of research go back to some of the important philosophical ideas that have influenced Western thought. Bryman (2004, p11) considers that the emphasis that is placed upon scientific practice within the normative perspective goes back to the ideas of the Enlightenment. This idea is central to the normative model of research so it can be claimed that the perspective has its intellectual origins in this classical thought. The interpretivist research paradigm emphasises the importance of individuals establishing creative meaning with the social world. Bryman (2004, p13) equates this approach to research with 'phenomenology'. This in turn links the perspective to the ideas within humanism and interactionism. In other words the genesis of the perspective's dominant idea can be linked to these theoretical perspectives. A summary of each of the three research perspectives follows. A definition of each of the key perspectives is given. Key figures influencing the perspective are identified and central terms within each perspective are explained.

Normative research

The normative model of research is based on scientific principles. David Hume is associated with this perspective. This research model tends to be grounded in measurable or 'statistical' data. This means that the perspective is based on precise measurements that test theoretical perspectives by applying reason to identify whether or not the theory can be proven or not. Research that is based on this perspective usually begins with a hypothesis proposing a correlation or relationship. The objective of the subsequent research process is to identify whether or not the hypothesis is correct. This then enables the researcher to produce broad generalisations that allow scientific theory to be generated.

Applying normative research to Early Years

Normative research is often used to reveal what is happening in the lives of children and families in the UK. There are numerous examples of where statistics are used to either prove or disprove an argument. Examples include the House of Commons Work and Pensions findings of 2003–2004 revealing that 8 per cent of UK children do not have a warm waterproof coat. These findings are quantified in a 'scientific' way in order to answer a hypothesis. A frequent strategy within this normative approach is to present statistical findings in combinations so that a set of statistics appear to be reinforcing an answer to a hypothesis. In the above example, other statistics are used to support the argument that poverty is a significant issue affecting many UK children and families. The report goes on to cite that '20 per cent of UK children live in poverty for over three years'. These statistics are used to present a definite answer to an aspect of research. They are statistics that are used to present a large scale general answer to question.

Interpretive research

Interpretivist research places an emphasis upon the importance of interpreting human experience. The perspective has been popularised by Edmund Husserl. In many respects the perspective is opposed to the normative model of research. Instead of emphasising the importance of 'scientific analysis', 'hypotheses' and 'surveys', interpretive research focuses on individuals and how they experience the social world. This means that data-gathering is regarded as reflecting the researcher's personal engagement with the research process. The process becomes as important as the data that has been gathered as there is the acknowledgement of the creativity of both the researcher and the research subjects. The consequence of this approach is that research becomes more narrative and less statistical.

Applying interpretive research to Early Years

In his (1993) book *Local Knowledge*, Clifford Geertz argues that 'largeness of mind' comes from reflecting on how we interact with others. This process of reflecting on interaction is at the centre of the interpretivist approach to methodology. It can be argued that some of the most profound accounts of Early Years have come from the interpretive model of doing research. This is revealed in Green and Hogan's (2005) book *Researching children's experience: approaches and methods*. The book is grounded in important themes such as 'anthropological and sociological perspectives', 'ethnographic research methods', and 'phenomenological approaches to research with children'. The authors do acknowledge that the normative approach to research is also important. As Green and Hogan say (2005, p5) 'if we want to know how many children have experienced the death of a parent we must collect appropriate statistics'. It is, however, implied that a statistical focus may not account for the rich variety of experience within the Early Years context. It can be suggested that this is a particularly important benefit of the interpretive approach to research. The creativity of children and Early Years practitioners may be captured by placing an emphasis on researching the process of interaction.

Action research

This research perspective has been popularised by Kurt Lewin. The central purpose of action research is to improve professional practice through researching into aspects of 'best practice'. Action research is developmental because the central aim of the research is to investigate practice with a view to developing professional roles. This means that action research does not attempt to discover general findings. It is research that is characterised by findings that are 'particular' and 'specific'. Action research is one of the most important forms of professional research. It is a research process that has been described as being 'cyclical' and not linear. This is because the research process involves data-gathering, reviewing the data that has been collected, planning for new action and in turn implementing new action.

Applying action research to Early Years

Action Research can be applied to Early Years by reflecting on professional practice. If there are elements of practice that are not working it is possible to research what needs to be done to make improvements to this situation. It is also possible to identify the aspects of professional practice that are working well in order to inform future professional work. As the Early Years context is an area of education that can be characterised by innovative government policy initiatives it appears to be constantly adapting to the latest inter-pretation of 'best practice'. This means that it is important to have action researchers who can inform and influence future policy initiatives.

REFLECTIVE TASK

Which of these research approaches do you think is the best approach to adopt as a researcher?

FEEDBACK

The answer to this question is that the approach that is adopted depends upon the nature of your research question. If you are doing research on the number of children under seven years of age who have experienced family breakdown, it may be more appropriate to adopt a normative approach in order to gather statistics so that a 'large-scale' analysis can be completed. This is not to say that this research question could not be answered by a smaller-scale focus that looks at the experiences of a few research participants. The approach that is adopted depends upon what the researcher wants to answer and how they want to respond to the research question. It may be that a combination of methods is used so that as well as gathering statistics there are also reflective accounts that are interpretive. In other words the different research models are not necessarily opposed to one another. They can be used together to produce a comprehensive answer to the research question.

The research methods

Research methods gather data that is either qualitative (non-statistical) or quantitative (statistical) or a combination of both. If you are doing research, a range of methods is available to you. The methods that you will use for your research depend upon the nature of the research question you want to answer. If you have a small-scale area of focus you are likely to use fewer data-collection methods. This may mean that you are inclined to use interpretive methods for gathering your data because you do not want to provide broad generalisations from your research. In other words the research perspective that is adopted and the methods that are used are entirely driven by the research question and its associated objectives.

In general, the normative approach is considered to be a structured scientific approach. This means that a deductive approach is adopted that tests a specific hypothesis. The research process is concerned with exploring the relationships that exist between particular variables. If one adopts this research perspective it is likely that the methods that are chosen are those that can gather large amounts of statistical data that can be quantified and used as a basis for broad conclusions.

In contrast, the research methods that are used within the interpretive perspective are relatively unstructured. The research is more likely to be 'inductive' or open-ended in nature. The research methods are concerned with identifying the meaning of social interaction. These 'negotiated meanings' are used to establish theories that attempt to explain social interaction.

Example research methods

A number of research methods are available to researchers. The previous section has identified that the type of methods that are used for data gathering depend on the nature of the research question. Some of the popular data gathering techniques are discussed in this next section.

Experiments
This type of data collection method is used within the normative model of research. Experiments adopt a 'cause and effect' approach by seeking to prove or disprove a hypothesis.

Surveys
Surveys are used in order to 'pool' or obtain information about attitudes, beliefs and behaviours. Surveys are usually large-scale and they tend to be associated with the normative perspective and its attempt to answer a research question in a 'scientific' manner.

Focus groups
Kreuger (1994) defines focus groups as being small structured groups (between four to 12 people) that are facilitated by the researcher. The aim of the focus group is to generate detailed discussion about an issue of relevance to the research question. This data is

gathered via a semi-structured question and answer discussion. Kreuger (1994) emphasises the importance of providing a permissive and non-threatening environment in order to generate detailed data.

Interviews

Gillham (2000) defines an interview as a conversation between two people in which the interviewer seeks particular responses from the interviewee. There are different types of interview. There are structured interviews that are rigidly structured, with a set of questions that all the interviewees are expected to answer. There are semi-structured interviews where a series of prompts are used with the interviewees in order to facilitate more flexible discussion about particular issues. There are also unstructured interviews where the discussion is about an area of focus with no prior prompts provided by the interviewer.

Observation

As well as there being different sorts of interviews, there are also different forms of observation. We can distinguish between between 'participant' and 'structured' observation. Structured observation is defined as being a quantitative analysis of actions whereas participant observation is regarded as being a qualitative engagement in interaction. In other words the type of observation that is done will link to the research paradigm that is being adopted by the researcher.

REFLECTIVE TASK

What are the advantages and disadvantages of questionnaires and interviews?

FEEDBACK

All of the above research methods have advantages and disadvantages. The methods that are used depend upon the research question that has been selected and the research objectives.

Questionnaires have the advantage of being able to gather quantitative and qualitative data. This is possible if you have a combination of closed and open questions. The 'yes/no' closed questions can be used to produce statistical data. The 'open' questions that request the views and opinions of research subjects can be used to gather qualitative data. Another advantage of questionnaires is that they can be issued to a large number of research subjects. If the questionnaire is well-designed this can mean that a large amount of data is gathered relatively quickly. Many students doing research find that a questionnaire is a useful way of beginning a research study. There is the possibility of gathering much initial data about the chosen area of study.

A disadvantage of questionnaires is that the questions can be misinterpreted by the research subjects. This means that it is important to ensure that the questions are written in a clear and unambiguous way. It is also important to ensure that the questions are organised in a logical way so that the research subjects can understand the rationale behind the questionnaire's design.

Interviews have the advantage of providing potentially 'rich' and detailed information about the research topic. If a researcher is interviewing a research subject for half an hour there is the possibility of gathering much data. It is also possible to treat the interviewee as an 'individual' so their views and opinions are respected during the research process.

A disadvantage of interviews is that they are potentially time-consuming. This means that you are unlikely to gather a large number of respondent views in a typical interview schedule. This in turn means that the research becomes small-scale and localised. It may then be impossible to establish a general theory that can be applied on a broad scale. Another potential disadvantage of the interview process is the influence of the interviewer on the interviewee. The interviewee may give answers to 'please' the interviewer as opposed to really saying what they think about particular issues.

Analysing data

We have previously identified that there are quantitative (or statistical) and qualitative (non-statistical) sets of data. Once the data has been gathered it needs to be analysed. This section of the chapter outlines some of the important aspects of the data analysing process.

Two example strands of data processing include 'quantitative data analysis' and 'qualitative data analysis'. Within quantitative data analysis we can distinguish between 'descriptive' and 'inferential' statistics. Whereas descriptive statistics identify the nature of the data findings, inferential statistics are used to generate theory from statistical data. Within qualitative data analysis we can use what is referred to as 'theme analysis' to generate theory from the qualitative data.

Descriptive statistics

Descriptive statistics are used to describe the numerical data that has been gathered. It makes sense that the first step in any statistical analysis is to describe the data that has been obtained. There are different types of descriptive statistics and these include frequency distributions; measures of central tendency; and measures of dispersion.

Frequency distributions
These descriptive statistics are used to describe the frequency of particular categories within a data set. This is exemplified in the subsequent table.

Table 6.3 Frequency distributions

Social class	Frequency	Percentage
1	7	17.5
2	15	37.5
3	8	20
4	6	15
5	4	10
Total	40	100

Measures of central tendency

These descriptive statistics provide a single figure to represent a data set as effectively as possible. Three popular ways of doing this are by presenting a 'mode', a 'median' and a 'mean'. The mode represents the most frequently occurring statistic, the median is the middle score in the data set and the mean is the arithmetic average score within a data set.

Measures of dispersion

Numerical data sets have differing degrees of internal variability. This means that each set of numerical data can differ according to the range that has been obtained. The 'range' in this instance refers to the highest and lowest scores within a set of data. An important term within this category of statistical analysis is 'standard deviation'. This term can be used to indicate how close or otherwise the statistical findings are to the average value. If you report that '68 per cent of all measurements fall within 1 standard deviation of the average' this indicates how close the data set is to the average value that has been obtained. In other words if the average was '9' this would mean that 68 per cent of the findings are between 7 and 10.

Inferential statistics

These statistics differ from descriptive statistics because they are used to generate theory as opposed to report findings. Inferential statistics look for the differences and the relationships between sets of data. These differences and relationships are then used to generate interpretations of the data. Alan Bryman (1997, pp4–5) defines inferential statistics as enabling the researcher to demonstrate that the results from a sample of the data set are likely to be found in any other random sample of the data.

Levels of measurement

Within statistical data sets there are four different levels of measurement that are used to interpret the information that has been gathered. These levels of measurement are referred to as 'nominal, ordinal, interval and ratio' measurements.

Nominal measurement

This term refers to measurements that are arranged according to categories. An example of nominal measurement can be seen with the following example of social class and its division into upper class, upper middle class, middle class, lower middle class, upper working class and lower working class.

Ordinal measurement

Ordinal measurement allows the data to be arranged in a numbered series. An example of ordinal measurement occurs if the respondents' attitudes are measured, with '1' representing 'most popular', '2' representing 'neutral' and '3' representing 'least popular'.

Interval measurement

This form of measurement has equal intervals between the points on the measurement scale. If you use whole numbers to present your statistical data you are using interval measurement as the basis of your theoretical conclusions. An example of this type of measurement is temperature where the range might be from −20 to 30 degrees centigrade. If you were researching how climate differences influence types of play on a global scale you might use interval measurement to present your findings.

Ratio measurement

This type of measurement is similar to interval measurement but it takes into consideration the intervals on the measurement scale in relation to 'absolute zero'. An example of ratio measurement can be seen with test scores where they are understood in relation to a score between 0 and 100.

Level of measurement and graphs

The type of measurement that is chosen in turn influences how the data should be presented. This is outlined in the following table:

Table 6.4 Type of measurement and choice of graph

Type of measurement	Pie chart	Bar chart	Scattergram
Nominal	*	*	
Ordinal	*	*	*
Interval			*
Ratio			*

Pie charts, bar charts and scattergrams

Using charts to present your findings can be an effective way of presenting the data that you have obtained. The subsequent section gives three examples of a pie chart, a bar chart and a scattergram.

Example pie chart

Number of respondents

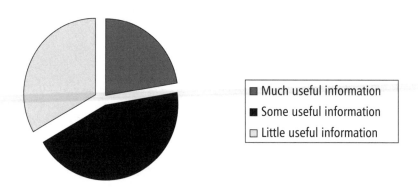

- ■ Much useful information
- ■ Some useful information
- □ Little useful information

Example bar chart

Number of respondents

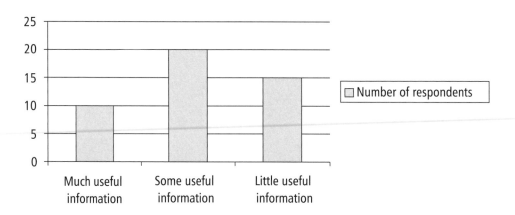

□ Number of respondents

Example scattergram

Average temperature of selected countries

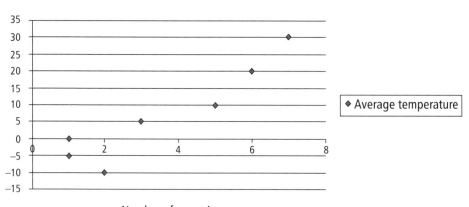

◆ Average temperature

Number of countries

Qualitative data analysis

The first stage in analysing qualitative data is to describe the data. You might want to present the main research findings and then write a paragraph about each of these main findings. By doing this you will be developing what Geertz (1973) refers to as 'thick description'. This means that you are developing thorough and comprehensive descriptions of the phenomena that are being studied. This 'thick description' gets its label from the depth of detail that is included about context, intentions, meanings and process.

Once the data has been described, it is possible to classify your findings, or in other words break the data down and put it back together in a meaningful way. This might mean that you have to develop categories in order to organise and classify your data. Categorising or classifying data enables you to 'funnel' your findings so that concepts can be compared and contrasted. This then enables you to look for patterns in the data that can be used to inform your theory. It provides you with the opportunity to explore the links that exist between categories. This in turn allows you to develop explanations that can explain these associations. Once you have analysed your qualitative data in this way you can then develop theory from your data.

REFLECTIVE TASK

Think about each of the stages of the research process and suggest how you might investigate attitudes to 'healthy eating' within a local primary school.

FEEDBACK

One of the most important parts of the research process is to choose a manageable research focus. You can do this through thinking carefully about the title of your research. In the above example, it is important to show that you are not going to embark on a research project that is too big and unmanageable. If you have a title like 'Critical appraisal of attitudes towards healthy eating in a local primary school' you have a manageable focus for your research because you are doing your research on one organisation. It is also important to ensure that your research objectives are manageable and that they show that you are aware of the importance of 'identifying, analysing and critically assessing' relevant issues. Never have too many objectives as it is hard to show that all the objectives have been achieved. In the above example research question you might have the following three research objectives.

- *Identify attitudes to healthy eating in a local primary school.*
- *Analyse attitudes to healthy eating in a local primary school.*
- *Appraise attitudes to healthy eating in a local primary school.*

Before beginning the research, you need to think about the research paradigm that will be applied to your study. In the above example question, all three of the research paradigms that we have referred to in the chapter are relevant to the question. This is because it is possible to gather statistics about healthy eating so the normative model of

FEEDBACK *continued*

research is relevant. In identifying 'attitudes', the interpretive paradigm is being applied. If the research findings are being used to make recommendations about how practice can be improved in the future, we can also say that the research question links to 'action research'.

Once you have identified your research paradigm, you need to think about how you will gather your data. The above research question can be answered through applying a combination of quantitative and qualitative data. You could design a questionnaire that has both closed and open questions in order to gather statistical and non-statistical data. The closed questions, with their 'yes/no' responses can be quantified. If you have a question like 'have you worked in the school for les than five years?' you can give a descriptive statistic that summarises this finding within your research report. If you include an open question such as 'what are your views on healthy eating?' you can in turn provide the attitudes and views of your respondents. In order to show that you are aware of the importance of triangulation you could develop this initial questionnaire into a series of semi-structured interviews with five of the respondents who completed the questionnaire. You could also do secondary research on the Internet to find out about other published accounts that link to your own research. This will help the validity and reliability of your findings. If you also show that all your research participants have had their confidentiality respected you can also say that you are aware of the importance of ethical principles.

PRACTICAL TASK

When you are in an Early Years setting take a research diary and make a note of which aspects of practice could be studied as an example of action research. Think about what you would need to do so that the research was valid and reliable.

We can now complete the chapter by focusing our discussion on critically appraising the research process by thinking about its value for Early Years.

Critical appraisal of the research process

The sort of research model that you use and the methods that are applied to your research are, as we have emphasised, determined by the nature of your research question and your research objectives. It is also important to consider the advantages and disadvantages of the different research models and methods.

Appraising normative research

The normative model of research has the advantage of being a large-scale approach to answering the research question. The surveys and experiments that are conducted within this research framework will typically generate much data that can be arranged to present a seemingly formidable answer. Another advantage of this approach to research is the emphasis that is placed on being 'objective' and 'scientific'. Bryman (2004, p11) argues that within this perspective, the research must always be conducted in a way that is 'value free'. A further advantage of the scientific nature of the normative approach is the 'definite' nature of the findings. Through applying statistics, you are able to give a definite answer to your research question. In appraising the value of the normative approach to research Bryman (2004, p13) argues that a difficulty with this research model rests with the confusion over the difference between the normative perspective and scientific research. In other words, is this model of research the same as 'scientific philosophy' or different? If the research model is different, how does it differ? Bryman also suggests that it is also not clear whether it is appropriate to study 'society' in a scientific way. This is because human beings interact in ways that are often contrary to the scientific model of the world.

Appraising interpretive research

The interpretive model of research places an emphasis on the 'phenomenology' of human experience. Bryman (2004, p13) summarises this idea as 'a philosophy that is concerned with the question of how individuals make sense of the world around them and how in particular the philosopher should bracket out preconceptions in his or her grasp of the world'. An advantage of this model of research is the attention that is given to the creativity of the research process. This means that interpretivism argues that researching human beings is an entirely different process to 'scientific research'. As opposed to looking for large-scale general theories, the researcher is looking at small-scale interpretations of social meaning. The advantage of this approach is that it is possible to recognise the profound nature of human interaction. This suggests that a scientific approach, with its emphasis on 'reason' and 'rationality', may miss the creative and inventive nature of human interaction. A difficulty of this model of research is seen in the Geertz (1988, p2) quote that the research process can become akin to 'the lady sawn in half' that is 'done but never really done at all'. As a result of the emphasis that is placed upon 'interpretation' the intensity of the research process can mean that the research findings are so localised and small-scale that it is impossible to generate any general theory. This point is reinforced by Bryman (2004, p16) who argues that interpretivist research represents 'tendencies rather than definite points of correspondence'. If this argument is developed you can challenge any interpretive research by claiming that the findings are representative of 'views and opinions' but little else. This can mean that it becomes difficult to generate theory from the research findings because of their small-scale, intense, and localised nature.

Appraising action research

Action research can appear to be a diverse and broad approach to the research process. This is acknowledged by Bryman (2004, p277). This can mean that the researcher becomes a central part of the field of study. The advantage of this characteristic of action research, is that it enables the collection of 'rich' data about the chosen topic. Paulo Freire (1970) draws attention to the impact that action research has had on developing educational practice. The cyclical nature of the action research process also means that the research model is not 'linear'. It is opposed to the 'thesis, antithesis, synthesis' model of thought that appears to have influenced the normative and interpretive research models. This means that there is the possibility of constantly comparing research findings as the emphasis is placed on gathering as much data as possible in order to inform future practice. Chambers (1983) draws attention to a difficulty with the action research process as a result of its inherently political nature. The researcher is intimately connected with the research process as a practitioner in the area of research. This can mean that it becomes difficult to gain an impartial view.

Appraising quantitative research

We have said that 'methodology' refers to the model of research that you are using and the data-collection methods that are being applied to answer the research question. Each data-collection method has advantages and disadvantages. Bryman (2004, p62) defines quantitative research as 'entailing the collection of numerical data'. An advantage of having quantitative data is that it can be used to generate statistical findings that appear to offer definite answers to specific research questions. If you read a research report and it states that '80 per cent of UK children aged 7–8 enjoy school' this appears to be a clear and unambiguous finding. Bryman (2004, p78) does, however, criticise quantitative researchers because 'they fail to distinguish people and social institutions from the world of nature'. This is because the processes that are used in analysing the social world are no different from those that are being used to analyse the natural world. We have already said that human beings have the capacity for inventiveness and creativity. This can mean that a statistical analysis of human behaviour does not account for every aspect of human interaction. This leads Bryman (2004, p78) to propose that quantitative measurement 'possesses an artificial and spurious sense of precision and accuracy'. It can also lead to a somewhat static portrayal of human life as the analysis is structured by statistics. Although it would be wrong to say that quantitative research is 'wrong' these criticisms need to be taken into consideration if you are adopting a quantitative approach to your research question.

Appraising qualitative research

Qualitative research is characterised by its focus on non-statistical data. Bryman (2004, p266) defines qualitative research as being 'concerned with words rather than with numbers'. We have said that an advantage of this approach is that it embraces the creativity of the research process. This means that the research process is understood in relation to 'negotiated meanings'. Qualitative research accounts can be detailed, enjoyable accounts that outline the interaction between the researcher and the research subjects. The criticisms of this process are made because of the difficulty that occurs if you want to develop general theory from a small-scale qualitative analysis. Bryman (2004, p284) argues that qualitative research can be 'too subjective'. This can mean that it becomes difficult to replicate a qualitative study because the research process is so particular to the area of study. This in turn means that it is very hard to generalise and give coherent answers to large-scale research questions. The involvement of the researcher within the research process can also mean that it is difficult to see what the researcher actually did and how the conclusions of the research were reached.

This chapter has given an outline of the research process by considering research in relation to Early Years. Doing research may not be 'easy' but it is not an impossible challenge. The secret of successful research appears to be being prepared. As opposed to doing 'hasty research' it is important to consider which model of research you are going to apply and which research methods you are going to use in order to gather your data. These approaches will be determined by your research question and its associated objectives. The rest of the research process resembles providing the evidence necessary to win an argument. You need to gather enough data to produce an answer that is reliable and valid. For the validity or authenticity of your data to be accepted you need to make sure that you are aware of the ethics of research. Always ensure that no harm results from your research. If these guidelines are followed doing research can be one of the most enjoyable aspects of Early Years. It is also one of the most important ways of understanding the Early Years context. This makes doing research especially relevant to an EYP.

Self-assessment questions

1 What are the names of three research models that are relevant to Early Years?

2 How can Early Years workers apply the research process to help children and maximise their professional practice?

3 Give an example strength and weakness of each of the three research models outlined in this chapter.

Moving on

This chapter has introduced you to the research process. Try to think of a research question and research objectives that would link to one of the main chapters in the book.

REFERENCES

Bryman, A. (2004) *Social research methods*. Oxford: Oxford University Press.

Bryman, A. and Cramer, D. (1997) *Quantitative data analysis: a guide for social scientists*. London: Routledge.

Chambers, R. (1983) *Rural development: putting the last first*. London: Longman.

Denzin, N.K. and Lincoln, Y. (2000) *The handbook of qualitative research*. Thousand Oaks, CA: Sage.

Freire, P. (1970) *Pedagogy of the oppressed*. London: Continuum.

Gillham, B. (2000) *Case study research methods*. London: Continuum.

Geertz, C. (1973) *The interpretation of cultures: selected essays*. New York: Basic Books.

Geertz, C. (1988) *Works and lives: the anthropologist as author*. Stanford. CA: Stanford University Press.

Geertz, C. (1993) *Local knowledge: further essays in interpretive anthropology*. London: Fontana Press.

Green, S. and Hogan, D. (2005) *Researching children's experience: approaches and methods*. London: Sage Publications.

House of Commons Work and Pensions Committee (Online: www. publications.parliament.uk).

Kreuger, R. (1994) *Moderating focus groups*. Thousand Oaks, CA: Sage.

Online dictionary. Online: (www.dictionary.reference.com).

Opie, L. (2004) *Doing educational research: a guide to first time researchers.* London: Sage.

Online dictionary. Online: (www.dictionary.reference.com).

FURTHER READING

Bryman, A. (2004) *Social research methods*. Oxford: Oxford University Press.
An excellent book giving a detailed account of the research process but the material is not always related to Early Years contexts.

Conclusion

This book has been written for Early Years professionals who need to develop their skills by applying academic concepts to professional practice. It can be argued that social science provides a number of potential explanations for complex aspects of human behaviour. This is one of the reasons why subjects such as psychology, sociology and social policy are such an integral part of the Early Years academic syllabus. Each of the main chapters has referred to the core elements of the EYPS benchmarks. These 'standards' represent one of the ways of reinforcing professional status within Early Years.

Book structure

The book has adopted an interactive approach by using activities and considering case studies in each of the main chapters. This is to ensure that the main themes are applied to specific Early Years contexts. Each of the chapters has attempted to engage the reader with issues that are of importance to Early Years. It is hoped that this book is more than a general social science textbook because the content places social science within the everyday context of Early Years practice.

The book's chapters have concentrated upon particular aspects of social science in relation to Early Years. Chapter 1 applies psychology to the Early Years context. The differing schools of psychological thought have been considered alongside working with children and families. Whereas behaviourist psychologists such as Skinner have emphasised the importance of external environmental factors in producing thoughts, humanists such as Rogers have placed an emphasis upon the importance of unique individuals processing thoughts that have been generated by the environment in a highly original way. It was argued that it is important to adopt as holistic an approach to psychology as possible if the subject is to be applied to Early Years. The therapies that are offered to Early Years professional practice from each perspective of psychology have merits that depend upon the particular context within which the therapies are being applied. Moreover, this holistic approach to applying psychological therapies to Early Years appears to support collaborative provision and multiagency working. It can be argued that this is an important policy theme within Early Years practice in general.

Chapter 2 has explored the application of sociology to the Early Years context. The ideas within sociological perspectives such as functionalism, interactionism and conflict theory have been considered in developing the argument that social factors are particularly important for children's growth and development. The application of sociology to the Early Years context has been considered through exemplification and critical appraisal of sociological perspectives in relation to Early Years.

Chapter 3 has discussed the importance of social policy for Early Years. The chapter has explained what social policy is, alongside analysing how social policy impacts upon the work of Early Years professionals. The chapter also offers a critical appraisal of the implications of selected social policies for Early Years practice. This means that it is important to be aware of the key social policy legislation that shapes the Early Years context. We argued that a key theme is the emphasis that is placed on partnership and collaborative working. This means that the ideal is for all the Early Years sectors to work together to help find what we referred to as 'joined-up solutions to joined-up problems'. We also argued that the emphasis that is placed on 'partnership' and 'working together' assumes that this model of practice is possible. It can be argued that the deep-seated social divisions that can characterise UK society may mean that a model of partnership and working collaboration becomes more of an 'ideal' than a 'reality'. The effectiveness of current government policy directions can be considered in view of this.

Chapter 4 has identified and discussed some of the issues that are associated with literacy and learning in Early Years. The chapter has focused on how children's learning develops with experience. A main theme of the chapter has been that the child's personality, thought processes and linguistic ability develop over time. This means that it is important for Early Years professionals to place children's development within context. We have argued that we cannot explain child development by focusing on one factor. A number of important experiences appear to influence the child's ability to learn. We also argued that it is important to adopt the holistic approach to child development that was recommended in Chapter 2. In other words, as opposed to regarding child development as being influenced by either 'biology' or 'social factors', it is important to accept that there are a combination of psycho-social and biological factors that appear to influence children's development. As opposed to adopting an 'either/or' approach to child development we need to adopt as broad a perspective as possible.

Chapter 5 has discussed the different experiences of childhood that appear in other places at other times. We argued that childhood differs according to time and place. In other words, the experience of childhood in the UK differs according to historical and cultural factors. The chapter also reveals that other cultures can have very different interpretations of the family and childhood. This means that children's experience of childhood is influenced by social communities. After discussing the importance of 'time and place', the chapter looked at UK society and discussed some of the current social issues that are affecting children and families in the UK today.

The final chapter has discussed research methods for EYPS. After identifying what the term 'research' means, we analysed ways that the research process can be used by Early Years practitioners. We identified that there are different research models and methods. We also argued that the type of research models and methods used in a research project will depend upon the nature of the research question. It can be argued that research is one of the most important aspects of academic work within Early Years. We need to conduct research into professional practice in order to identify how the profession can move forward. This means that the design of our research question and its associated methodology become critical to the process of identifying what needs to be changed within Early Years professional practice.

The book aims to make a contribution to enhancing the professional development of Early Years professionals. If this occurs it will achieve the highest of aims. There cannot be a more important professional role than helping children to develop. After all, today's children are tomorrow's adults and they represent the social future for generations to come.

Appendix: Answers to self-assessment questions

Chapter 1

1 The five major schools of psychology are: psychoanalytical, behaviourist, humanistic, neurobiological and cognitive.

2 The best way of applying psychology to Early Years is through holistic therapies that combine the principles of behaviourism, humanism, cognitive, psychodynamic and neurobiological psychology to meeting the complex needs of individuals.

3 *Table 1.2 Schools of psychology*

School of thought	Strength	Weakness
Behaviourism	Acknowledgement of environmental influences on the mind.	A tendency to neglect individual creativity with external factors.
Humanism	Acknowledgement of how individuals manipulate external variables.	Rogerian theory is idealistic.
Psychodynamic	Acknowledgement of the workings of the unconscious mind.	The theory is not methodologically proven.
Cognitive	Acknowledgement of the different thought processes during human cognitive development.	The idea of stages of development is not necessarily the case. Cognitive development is more a process than a series of stages.
Neurobiological	Acknowledgement of the link between human thoughts and hormones/chromosomes.	The theory is biologically reductionist.

Chapter 2

1 Three influential sociological perspectives are functionalism, interactionism and conflict theory.

2 The best way of applying sociology to Early Years is through combining the perspectives with psychological therapies in order to meet the complex needs of children and families.

3 *Table 2.2 Schools of sociology*

School of thought	Strength	Weakness
Functionalism	Acknowledgement of the importance of the social system.	A tendency to neglect individuals who negotiate social meanings.
Interactionism	Acknowledgement of the importance of creative individuals generating social meanings.	A tendency to focus on the role of individuals to the detriment of wider social structures.
Conflict Theory	Acknowledgement of the importance of economics.	A tendency to reduce social factors to economic variables

Chapter 3

1 New Labour's key policy theme is 'partnership'.

2 Three examples of New Labour policy affecting Early Years are Every Child Matters, mentoring and multiple intelligences.

3 A strength of New Labour is the importance that is given to statutory services. A weakness of the emphasis on partnership is that it is difficult to be 'all things to all people'. To apply the familiar saying, it is impossible to please all of the people most of the time.

Chapter 4

1 The main psychological perspectives accounting for the development of the child's personality are behaviourism, humanism, psychodynamic theory, cognitive theory, and biological psychology. These perspectives can be combined with the sociological perspectives that are outlined in chapter 2 to give a detailed explanation of children's linguistic and learning development.

2 Malim and Birch (1998, p468) argue that both Piaget and Vygotsky accept the fundamental importance of the child interacting with its environment if cognitive development is to occur. The difference may be considered as being how the two psychologists are perceived. Whereas Piaget is characterised as placing an emphasis

upon stages of cognitive development, Vygotsky is remembered for his notion of a 'scaffold' of influential peers influencing cognitive thought processes. It is important to acknowledge that although the two psychologists may have a difference in focus this does not necessarily mean that they are diametrically opposed to one another.

3   It can be argued that it is too simplistic to argue that a child's personality is a product of either its biology or its social circumstances. It is more effective to acknowledge that personality development is a complex combination of social, environmental and biological variables. This view is supported by writers such as Richard Gross (2004) who argue against reducing personality development to one particular set of variables.

Chapter 5

1   The nuclear family is not universal. Kathleen Gough's (1962) research on the Nayar indicates that there are a variety of family types so we cannot say that all families are 'nuclear'.

2   Family form is influenced by 'history' and 'location' or 'time and place'.

3   Family breakdown appears to be one of the key factors influencing children's experience of childhood in the UK today.

Chapter 6

1   The three research models that are especially relevant to Early Years are the normative, interpretive and action research perspectives.

2   The best way of applying the research process to Early Years is through identifying a possible topic of 'action research' so that the research can be used to inform future professional practice.

3

Research model	Strength	Weakness
Normative	Acknowledgement of quantitative data.	A tendency to neglect individuals creating social meaning.
Interpretive	Acknowledgement of how individuals negotiate meaning.	Research is usually small-scale and localised.
Action Research	The research can be used to inform future professional practice.	It is difficult to be 'impartial' as an action researcher as you are intimately involved with the research process.

Index